# What People Are Saying About This Book

*" I beseech you to read this book. It grasped my attention from beginning to end. Lisa was the first social worker assigned to my home when I began my journey as a therapeutic foster parent over 23 years ago. Years later, she was the therapist for several children placed in my home. She was able to ignite a beam of light in each child giving them the opportunity to catch the moon. Whether you are a teacher, social worker, student, foster parent or a foster child, you will benefit from reading "Who Can Catch the Moon?" I was inspired and attained additional knowledge from reading this author's perspective-and it rejuvenated my moon. Grab hold of the information shared and it will ignite your moon as well.*

*Kudos Mazzeo!!!!!!!!! Thank you for sharing your perspective."*

**Sheila Wimbush Bowles, MS**
**Foster Parent Recruiter-Family and Children's Agency (Norwalk, CT)**
**Therapeutic Foster Parent**

*"Lisa Mazzeo captures her personal and professional insights both which are critical in order to be an effective and compassionate Child Welfare professional. "Who Can Catch the Moon?" illustrates her personal*

*journey and the way her life/work experiences impact who she is as a person and as a social worker."*
**Maria H. Brereton, MSW**
**Regional Administrator-State Department of Children and Families (DCF)**

*"Lisa shares her personal story and professional challenges...creating a "map' to guide workers in their journey towards increased clinical skills and the tender use of self to heal those who hurt."*
**MaryAnne Judge, LCSW**
**Former Staff Development and Training Manager-Casey Family Services**

*"Lisa Mazzeo is a very original voice that will be heard. She writes and speaks from her heart with great clarity, vision and delightful humor. She is a brilliant and wise therapist. This is a "must read" whether you are a professional, a parent, foster parent or general reader. She handles the basics with common sense and proven approaches. A great read!"*
**Debbie Tadduni, LCSW**
**Director of Foster Care-Family and Children's Agency (Norwalk, CT)**
**Therapeutic Foster Parent**

*"I believe in Lisa Mazzeo's message and tell clients at least once a week in my practice that your body can be hurt, your feelings can be hurt but your soul will never die and no one can take it away. That internal flame carries many of our clients even if the "light of the*

# Who Can Catch The Moon?

## Lisa A. Mazzeo, LCSW, BCD

*Heartfelt, humorous and compelling stories of resiliency in society's most vulnerable children*

www.TotalPublishingAndMedia.com

The moon's light is strong
and its glow fiercely ignites
the path we travel.
The power of the moon is eternal.
Even through cloud
light is possible
if you're brave enough to search it out.

moon" is dim in the world around them. Ms. Mazzeo shares her personal journey and her light in a way that all can understand and relate to. This book is not just for people in the profession, the general population needs to read these heartfelt accounts in order to understand the most neglected in this country: our children. "Who Can Catch the Moon?" so brilliantly shows that it takes all of us together to make a difference in the lives of children. Even one caring, interested, and nurturing person can do it as well-if they are willing to go the distance between here and the moon."

**Maria C. Castillo, L.C.S.W, contributing author in "Miracles Happen: The Transformational Healing Power of Past-Life Memories" by Brian L. Weiss, M.D. and Amy Weiss, M.S.W.**

"Although I technically don't fall into the target audience for Lisa Mazzeo's book "Who Can Catch the Moon?," I was not only touched by her words but also able to learn from them. Storytelling is one the most effective ways to teach, and through these poignant accounts there are not only lessons on parenting and guidance for children but also general life advice that would apply to anyone. This book serves as a reminder that even if we can't catch the moon we can all help those who have lost their way back to its healing light."
**Maggie Mellinger, BS**

"This is a book you just cannot put down. Throughout the book you'll experience Lisa's genuine sense of humor and personality through heartfelt and jaw

*dropping stories. Through a combination of personal and professional events, Lisa captures the reader and allows them to experience the relationships she has with children experiencing indescribable hardships. 10 years ago I was a client of Lisa's-Now I consider her family. Her dedication and love for all children is absolutely powerful and is illustrated throughout her story."*
**Jayme Felner, M.Ed**

*"Who Can Catch the Moon? By Lisa Mazzeo is a well written and thoughtful clinical prose that fully illustrates all facets involved in treating and caring for our traumatized children and adolescents. The use of self, humor, metaphor, skills, personal and professional experiences are all necessary to inspire hope and healing. Lisa, I thank you for sharing your insights."*
**Debra Bond, PhD, Licensed Clinical Psychologist, Colleague and Friend**

# Dedication

This book is dedicated, of course, to my parents. They are responsible for my perspective and the reason I consider myself a resilient person. Their positive approach to parenting helped me to view the world as a full place rather than an empty one. My parents provided me with opportunity and life provided me with luck. Together, the two brought me down a path words cannot fully capture.

My parents encouraged me to write down "my" experiences and if not for their constant suggestion, I might never have.

I dedicate this book to my brother Glenn Mazzeo, my sister in law Beth and to my niece Lindsay and nephew Luke.

I dedicate this book to my sister Debbie Boyum, my brother in law Steven and to my nieces Andrea and Amiee.

If not for the love and support of my family, my moon may never have been recognized.

I dedicate this book to every child, youth and family I have had the honor to meet. Each has taught me a little more about life, human nature, humor and resiliency.

# Table of Contents

# Why You Should Read this Book

Y ou should read this book if you are interested in children and learning how they move beyond horrendous experiences.

You should read this book because it addresses the many sides of social work, humanity and the ways in which we practice and understand our craft.

Lastly, you should read this book because it offers insight into the nuances of basic human development and how, despite tremendous odds, resiliency helps children grow into their full potential.

# Acknowledgements

A heartfelt thank you to Tracey Carter, M.Ed for writing "About the Author," Jen Crowley, LCSW for writing the book summary and Nanette Gamache for designing the cover.

Special thanks to Diane Kapinos who read the book and provided valuable feedback.

# Forward

When Lisa participated on child welfare task forces and in planning groups I led at Casey Family Services, I found her experience, insights and sense of humor to be invaluable. Reading her book, I would say these same qualities shape both the book's style and content, resulting in engrossing reading and making a valuable contribution to the child welfare field. Social workers, administrators, judges, attorneys, parents and anyone who works with children and youth will benefit and relate to Lisa's insights about her young clients, the system charged with their protection and care and from the questions she raises and the lessons she shares.

Professionals in the child welfare field will no doubt have read a plethora of books on child development, emotional and behavioral disorders, and therapeutic interventions. What makes this book so unique is its ability to make abstract theory come alive through true life examples of Lisa's interactions. Rarely do we have an opportunity to view the unfolding lives of vulnerable youth from the perspective of a professional helping them heal from past wounds and finding the strength to trust again.

It's ALL About the Relationship, the title of Chapter 4 sums up Lisa's belief about the utmost influence in shaping a child's life. A central theme of the book is one I concur with wholeheartedly both personally and professionally. Relationships with loving, nurturing, consistent caregivers and adults and the positive messages they provide to children are key to healthy development, self-confidence and a sense of security. Woven throughout the book is the juxtaposition of Lisa's growing up in a strong, nurturing, caring family and the experiences of the youth she encounters in her practice. Interactions with Lisa match her description of her family; caring, sincere, strong, intuitive, and honest to a fault. She is not afraid to share those instances where, despite her best efforts, she is unable to help a youth break through the limitations, fears and insecurities imposed by difficult histories, and a lack of nurturing caregivers. Her honesty is also apparent in how she responds to difficult questions and challenges posed by youth testing her sincerity or trying to make sense of their chaotic lives and fragile futures.

The compelling stories of Lisa's work with youth over the course of her career engage the reader and make it difficult to put the book down before its conclusion. Woven through these stories are psychological theories and constructs, attachment, resilience, brain development and trauma. These help explain the behavior and emotional challenges of youth growing up void the unconditional love and guidance of permanent, consistent caregivers. While child welfare professionals will relate to these concepts, drawing on their own knowledge and experience, the average reader will not be lost. Lisa's writing style makes you feel like you are sitting in her living room having a conversation. You will experience the intensity of her commitment to youth, her sense of humor, her curiosity about people, and her interest in lifelong learning.

Lisa draws attention to the important concept of resiliency in children. Evolving from her personal and professional experience, Lisa's views and definition of resiliency are consistent with research literature. Why do some children with difficult and tumultuous histories emerge as successful, caring adults, while others descend into further chaos and self-defeating behavior? As Lisa's insights suggest, somewhere along the line, the children who overcame the odds experienced a connection with a caring adult who made them feel worthwhile. Lisa's description of resilience as a lifejacket that keeps us afloat during difficult times, leads us to question and reflect on how we can insure that children have the caring adult connections that is key for developing resilience.

Lisa is not afraid to tackle controversial subjects. As an example, she raises the issue of professional boundaries, giving her perspective on and when to continue a connection with a client once the therapeutic relationship has terminated. Spirituality is another subject infrequently written about in professional literature. Lisa does not hesitate to share how her spirituality is integrated into her personal and professional life.

In my social work education no professor ever advised me to "find my groove" as a social worker. Lisa uses this humorous frame to raise awareness of the power of integrating one's unique and authentic self into professional practice. Lisa's description of how she initially "stumbled upon her style" consciously integrating her strengths, learning, intuition, and judgment into her professional approach can be particularly instructive to beginning therapists.

Lisa suggests that "our only responsibility to someone else is to be who we are. It's the best gift we can offer and it's genuine". She has offered honest reflections on her journey as a social worker in the child welfare system. The pain she has witnessed, a sense of hopelessness she has tried to dispel, mistakes she sees in hindsight and lives whose trajectories have changed as a result of her persistence and clinical instinct. It is rare to be given such an intimate view of the experiences of the child welfare professional. Lisa has revealed who she is by sharing her personal and professional story – it is the best gift she can offer.

Joy Duva, MSW
Assistant Executive Director-Former Casey Family Services
(Direct services arm of Annie E. Casey Foundation)

# Preface

*Literature ignites curiosity;*
*experiences fuel the fire.*

My perspective on life and what I believed to be true began to change in 1984. The changes came slowly and continue still today. Everything I had known to be honest and true had been challenged and before I knew it, life was nothing as I thought it was or would be.

In January of 1984, I accepted my first job as a social worker and this job came in the form of employment with the State of Connecticut Child Welfare Department. It was my most difficult job and proved to be my greatest opportunity for growth. Being young and naive, I couldn't have begun to imagine what this would mean for me both as a professional and personally. I didn't know what I didn't know and 30 years later, I still don't know.

In my role as an advocate for and protector of children, I learned poignant lessons and witnessed things that would make the average person question the fairness of the world in which we live. I sure did. My experiences have taught me life, in all of its greatness and sadness, presents us with challenging lessons for growth. At the time, I had no idea the profession to which I chose to dedicate my life, would lead me to evolve as an individual.

This book contains my experiences, my perspectives and my lessons, yet I believe the lessons to be universal. For this reason, I chose to share them.

Acknowledgment and gratitude were two of my first lessons as a young adult. I grew up in the safe confines of Fairfield, Connecticut, a town within a financially well-off county, less than an hour from New York City. The town of Fairfield is surrounded by Westport and Bridgeport. Both areas-the town and the city respectfully-are polar opposites of one another. One screams wealth and success while the other whimpers poverty and desperation. As a child and young adult, I had no idea the two could exist within miles of one another.

Diversity, cultural and the like, was not something I experienced growing up. I barely saw it at school and as I got older and entered the job force, I didn't see it there either. It wasn't until I went off to College I understood what true diversity represented. I graduated from Southern Connecticut State University, a university strategically placed right smack in the middle of New Haven. To further accentuate the point of polarity, the wealth of Yale University glistened and spread its wings in a city with high poverty and higher crime rates.

The reality of culture shock collided abruptly with my own perceptions and I was both astounded and confused, yet I tried to embrace the new challenge with interest and curiosity rather than fear and abandonment. My knowledge regarding the vast differences between people became further defined when I graduated and became employed. It was this exact moment where I began to appreciate all I was given as a child and teenager. As the differences continued to present themselves, I knew it must mean something more so I began to pay closer attention. I realized I was venturing down a new life path.

The next valuable lesson came when it became clear I needed to explore my moon; my resiliency. Resiliency is a fascinating concept to me and I began taking note of how some developed it and how others have trouble. I haven't done empirical research to back up my hypothesis on the subject but have come to realize that those who are resilient have become so because in their darkness, someone was there to offer a beacon of light. People represent the "light" and these good hearted, well-meaning and giving individuals offer it to others so darkness will not prevail. I have been given the gift of resilience and because I don't want to be part of a world where hope is lost, and where people feel worthless, I pass on this gift to those who need it. I want people, more specifically children, to feel prepared for life's challenges, regardless of what those challenges may be.

Lastly, I've learned people deserve compassion, love and understanding. They deserve to live a life without judgment from others. Without this basic societal value, no one experiences the light of moon.

# Introduction

It was a beautiful clear fall evening in 1994. I was driving down a rural road in lower Fairfield County, Connecticut. On any other day, it would have been a picture perfect evening. Beside me, a nine year old boy sat. In the midst of all this beauty, the daunting task of moving a child to his 11th foster home was before me. I began to speak as the radio quietly played in the background. The best communication with children takes place while driving but on this day, I'd be the one doing most of the talking.

As I began this all too familiar dialogue; the one where I try and explain why another home is necessary at this time, the heavy words were met with silence. Although child welfare social workers continuously try and find "just the right words" to break the bad news, the words never seem to be there. How can we be part of a system, which seems to do more harm than good? Letting a few minutes quietly pass, I turned and asked, "Do you have any questions about what I said?" With barely a thought he replied, "Yeah, *who can catch the moon?*" At that moment, my personal belief about resiliency in children rang true. In my world, his life was falling apart but in his world, life carried on as usual. I swallowed hard and continued driving, trying desperately to make sense of his response.

The idea to write a book was born from this brief life changing experience yet scribing out the thoughts did not happen as quickly. This book is an attempt to capture and share the many experiences I've had as part of the child welfare system. They have shaped who I am today-both personally and professionally-because the two are simply not mutually exclusive.

# Everything Starts at the Beginning

What makes a person trust, let alone a child filled with anxiety; innate fear and doubt trust another person? Questions like this beg response, thought and introspection and lead one to review one's own childhood and life trajectory when crafting a satiable answer. After all, we are who we are because of our life experiences. I ask myself what was it my parents did to cause me to never doubt my overall self-worth or physical and emotional safety-did they even know they were doing it?

They were consistent, caring, took charge, stood firm in a parental (rather than friend) role, never made me feel more powerful than them, gave me direction and went to work every day. They had strong egos, gave me independence, meant what they said, remained consistent in their messages and they cooked dinner every night and we ate together as a family. Sunday family dinners were a must (no choice on whether you would be there; you were there and you liked it). They gave punishments which fit the crime and showed me my father was the head of the household (when you crossed "the boundary" you knew you had pushed too hard) and taught me "the" look which meant I needed to shut my mouth and listen. Without ever knowing it, they were laying the foundation and providing the structure every single child needs; despite the child's ongoing fight against it. I've drawn from this structure every single day of my life. My parents relied on their own instincts and likely were parented well themselves. Our best teachers in life are typically right in front of us; whether or not we choose to listen is a completely different discussion.

My parents were not college educated people and worked hard for everything they had. They had street smarts and used their natural instincts often. My mother, the homemaker, seemed to know a lot about psychology to not be formally trained. I was the youngest of three. Each day my sister and brother would go off to school and since I wasn't yet of school age, I would stay home with my mother. I guess she could figure, from my less than subtle cues, I was sad about not going off with them so she invented a game we would play, just her and I. The game was called "Mrs. Brown and Mrs. Jones." Every morning both Mrs. Jones and Mrs. Brown would make the beds, vacuum the floors, dust the furniture, and straighten out the bathroom and kitchen. When we were all done with our chores, we would have our "coffee" and talk time. I thought this was the greatest game I ever played because I had my mother all to myself and it was our special together time. We had fun. We were together. I didn't have to share her with anyone. The world was a good place and my mother loved me! This was all I knew and was all I cared about. It wasn't until I took my first psychology course as a freshman in college I learned this little "game" was called reverse psychology. I remember calling my mother one evening to let her know the jig was surely up. She started laughing. She knew what I had just figured out; I was her free "house cleaning service!"

This and many exchanges like it helped me to feel secure, comforted and confident. I grew up never, ever having to question whether I was a loveable person; I already knew I was because my parents made sure I knew it. My parents parented using intuition, not books. Their parenting undoubtedly mirrored how they were parented when they were children. And, the cycle continues. If you learn by example and the lessons are repeated, the information becomes integrated and rote. It's second nature.

In 30 years of practice, I've probably treated hundreds of children; children who have come from diverse ethnic and socio-economic backgrounds, and varying family systems. I have been honored to work with children in foster care, residential care, who have been adopted and those who have been raised by their biological parents. Though some commonalities run through all, there are distinct differences which separate them. Their individual experiences have led them down a path our work together only begins to unravel. With basic trust and a solid therapeutic relationship, the journey begins and the one thing I know-with every fiber of who I am-is when a child feels as though a trustworthy adult has claimed and cared for them; dug their claws into them so to speak, their healing process begins. And so it goes...

In my work, I'm reminded constantly of those who failed to experience what I did growing up; a secure attachment to the people who loved me. I concur with the voluminous amounts of research which tell us the early years significantly set the stage for a lifetime and if developmental milestones, as psychoanalysts taught us, are not achieved completely, we keep redoing them until we get them right. I am aware, too, every person is born with a genetic blueprint and despite intervention this blueprint sometimes controls their individual journey.

As a social work undergraduate student, my immature brain challenged this statement when my professor introduced it. It sounded strange to me as I couldn't imagine an adult crawling around until he mastered the skill. What I have come to learn is it is not the crawling, per se, but the skills derived from the experience. Thank goodness or we would all look pretty foolish crawling on the floor each day! Essentially what we do is keep going back to moments in our lives when something went off track, and we keep repeating maladaptive behaviors until we understand why we are behaving in this way. This is the work of the therapist and the client. I believe the main purpose of therapy is to provide a "corrective experience" in a safe environment-with the purpose of healing. A solid and trusting relationship between therapist and client is imperative. Unfortunately, when most people enter therapy for the first time, they don't necessarily know this to be true and they begin by saying, "I'm here but I don't want you blaming my mother (father, grandmother, aunt or whoever the primary caretaker was) for my problems." Most want a quick fix but might not necessarily want to dive into the root causes and relive the pain. From my perspective, a degree of this must be done in order to understand what is happening in the present, yet cannot be rushed into without the relationship development.

I find the above "quick fix" theory to be true, more specifically, with parents of teenagers. They come seeking help for their child and are quick to "blame" their teen for acting out rather than looking at the contributing factors. Parents forget what their own teenage years were like.

I'm not a coddler by any means. My fundamental belief is people make choices in their lives and even those who misbehave choose to do so because it serves some purpose. I immediately begin thinking about root causes of misbehavior and underlying fears associated with such acting out. Not everyone is prepared to hear the "why" and most find they are only interested in the solution. I quickly try and assess why the teen feels the need to act out and thus disrupt the family. Questions race through my mind as I listen and assess what is going on in the here and now. The here and now will lead us to the beginning. The process isn't a quick one as all the pieces of the puzzle must seamlessly fit together in order to see the whole picture. Again, I'm cognizant not to jump too quickly because I realize the first therapeutic hurdle comes in the form of relationship building.

If we presume every behavior is rooted in fear, shouldn't the first question be, "What is this child afraid of?" The same holds true for the caregiver, "What is this parent afraid of?" The therapist's job is to listen to what is being said (and not said) and assess the total situation. Together we can then identify what is ***really*** happening. It is about making connections and observations for people with the goal of determining underlying causes. Once the cause of dysfunctional coping behavior is understood, we can begin the journey onward.

Whenever I meet someone for the first time, I can sense the discomfort and mistrust which is present. This is a normal response when strangers meet for the first time. We all go through a checklist in our minds as we assess the other person's trustworthiness. When they walk into my office, I not only see them but I see all the ghosts they carry with them as well. I use "ghosts" as a figurative term because each person carries with them the messages and experiences they have received all their lives from the people in their lives (who mattered most) and those messages play, nonstop, throughout their life cycle. Take the 17 year old girl who presents with low self-esteem, suicidal thoughts and self-mutilation. As far as I can see, she is a likeable, engaging, and pleasant person and I tell her so, yet in her mind she is convinced she isn't. Regardless of what I say, she believes only what she believes. She chooses, through bad behavior, to punish herself each day because subconsciously, she doesn't feel worthy of living or of love from others. She has been told, as far back as she can remember, everything she does is wrong. If I give her a compliment or praise her for something she has done correctly, she inevitably hears the negative and does not have trust in what I am saying as truthful. Why should she? It is a first time experience for her. The goal of our work is for her to learn how to hear what is being said, and to accept the positive like she would a breath of cleansing air. We are successful in our work if this response becomes rote and takes little thought on her part. Essentially, we have to erase the negative tapes of her childhood which play in her head (routinely) and replace them with positive messages so she can see herself differently and have a cathartic experience. Though it sounds fairly basic, the work takes time and absolute trust on the part of the client and the therapist. The relationship between the two has to be a solid one, without fear or judgment. Change is not easy for any of us and I recognize sticking with what is comfortable, even though it might ultimately be bad for you, is often the choice of many.

Trust is the fundamental building block for all solid relationships. Unfortunately, it is fiercely sought after but at times not always attained. People who lack the basic skill set needed to develop trust in others can spend an entire lifetime trying to learn how to find it and/or navigate it. This is a good time to tell you the story about my friend. She experienced ongoing trauma as a child. Though she had gone through years of psychotherapy to understand the wrongs experienced in her life, seeking out and maintaining strong, consistent relationships, as well as basic trust for others remain the obstacles for her to overcome.

We had been friends for several years and because my life experiences/upbringing dictated one way for me to react to certain situations in life and hers dictated the complete opposite I always marveled at how different our reactions were to the same situation. One night she came over for a visit. Prior to her coming, the neighbor's dog had taken an uninvited stroll through my house. I had *NO IDEA* the dog had decided to "do his business" in my front hallway. When my friend came over, she stepped right smack in the middle of the "little gift." The only warning I had something was wrong was when she yelled, "Who put this dog sh*t here?" When we finally stopped laughing, it occurred to me this was just another example of how basic trust in others plays a role in our everyday life. Why, in God's name, would I purposely leave dog remains in my front hallway for her to step in when I knew she was coming over but honestly, for a moment, she really thought I had. Why? Because she possessed a lack of basic trust for the relationship, her first instinct was to assume this was yet another example of my lack of honesty. This was a comical and very telling situation for both her and me.

Another friend (my best friend) and I met in college when we were 20. She called me one day to ask if I could tell the professor she wouldn't be in class for the next few days. I asked her if she was okay and she responded rather routinely, "Yes, my sister died yesterday." She reported this trauma laden, life changing experience completely removed from the emotional aspect of the situation. In other words, her reaction was inconsistent with the event. Raised in an Italian family, emotions were our seventh sense. They were as transparent to us as the day was long. Working from this baseline, the little exclamation point in my head screamed so loudly I was sure she heard it on the other end of the phone. Of course I'm thinking if this were my sibling, you'd be picking me up off the floor. I wouldn't be calm. I would be sobbing. I shockingly responded "Died, did you say she died? Are you okay?" Calmly my friend answered, "Yes, she was sick. I have to go to her funeral." We hung up the phone and I just stood there stunned by her lack of connection to the experience.

When she returned from the services days later I tracked her down to see how she was managing and I was met with the same removed type of response. This, I have to say, was foreign to me. As we got to know each other better, I learned my friend was raised in an Irish Catholic family. The Irish are known for keeping their emotions close to the chest. The outside world is rarely invited into the private part of who they are. She knew the behavior she was familiar with thus her response was normal, even though it was completely abnormal to me. So, is it a wonder every time she came to my house and was met with hugs and kisses she wanted to jump out of her skin? She probably yearned for a little more emotion in her life and I could have done with a little less. As life went on, we became best friends and she is the first to say she didn't really understand the closeness and unconditional love of a family until she became part of mine. Our friendship helped her understand what it meant to trust others.

Several years ago, I was fortunate enough to meet a wise young lady who had spent her childhood in foster care. Though she was fairly successful in her adult life-struggling but managing-she summed up her childhood metaphorically by saying "growing up in foster care was like being led around a forest blindfolded." There was no predictability and each day presented a new set of rules by which to live. Therefore, it wasn't surprising she had difficulty predicting what to expect next from people and why she felt anxious and defensive. For her, it was a simple matter of survival; she did what she needed to do in order to get by. She was the first to recognize she failed to learn the necessary skills to develop long-standing and meaningful relationships in her life. Solid role models and teachers were absent from her life because adults were interchangeable and no one, until much later in life, claimed her as theirs. She felt lost, unprepared and blindfolded most of her life.

These three stories illustrate how early experiences and messages shape who we are and how we respond to the world at large; I have heard variations of them often. For many, I included, they represent sad truths and define some people's lives. It's hard to reach out to others when no one consistently and unconditionally reaches out to you. It is a basic expectation, a right and a need for any person's development into an emotionally fulfilled and stable adult. Unless we recognize, understand and challenge this, it will haunt us forever.

The foundation of one's life helps create grounding. As we grow older, we depend on and rely on stable footing in order to continue building. When there are weaknesses or cracks in our early development, we can't adequately continue developing in an emotionally healthy manner.

# "Villages, Villages and MORE Villages"

*If we hold hands and gather in a circle, together, we celebrate*

G rowing up, my parents set up villages. We lived in suburban neighborhoods where every parent knew every child. If your parents weren't watching you then someone else's parents were and whatever you did, good or bad, was reported back to the mother ship and you heard about it (when you least expected). I learned my mother *really didn't* have eyes in the back of her head; just had loud-mouthed spies!

Aside from the natural connections found in healthy neighborhoods, my parents set up villages because they had good friends and supportive extended family. These friends became parental extensions of themselves. They were close enough to be considered family and they held the same power and responsibility for us as my own parents did. My parents reciprocated with their children. In essence, I had many mothers and many fathers and this was a good thing; a safe and comforting thing. We were loved and our sense of physical and emotional safety was never questioned. I believe my parents knew this instinctively and their innate wisdom proved successful.

To further "my village," I had caring teachers, some to whom I am still connected. I mention it here because

I remained in the same school system/same town throughout my educational years. It doesn't seem very noteworthy but this is another thing that can help you feel part of something greater. There is comfort in having people in your life who really know you and remind you that you are part of a larger whole. Many kids, especially those involved in the child welfare system, don't have the consistency of the same K-12 school system. This is not only unfortunate but a terrible disadvantage. With every new system, something gets lost in the translation, and consequently, the child's educational needs get lost as well.

When my "second" father Jimmy passed away a couple of years ago, I was asked to do the eulogy at his funeral. This has been the greatest honor of my life to date. Making him real to those who didn't know him as well as I did, was an awesome challenge. It is difficult to pay homage to someone who had more dimensions than words can describe. He was an artist, a writer, a storyteller, a comedian, a father, a husband and an exceptional friend-just to name of few.

The greatest gift Jimmy gave to "his" kids- his two biological children and the three of us-was his love. It was easy for him and it was evident. He loved and understood children with every fiber of his being. In his joking, kid-like and playful manner, Jimmy made you feel as though you were the only one in life who mattered. He always did things which made me feel valued and understood. I wasn't "just some kid," I was special. I have come to see him as a soul mate in this lifetime. When he and I walked on the beach-in absolute solace-he walked just far enough ahead so I wouldn't see he was dropping his coins onto the sand for me to find. I felt richer with each coin I found. He made me feel rich long after the walks were over. Throughout my life the lifelong impact of the message; "feeling rich" and loved and lucky…has been a special gift and recorded message hard wired into my brain. Parents like mine, the Jimmy's of the world and all others who value life, raise children who believe they are worth the air they breathe and the environmental space they fill. Sadly, some children are not given this gift. My village was large, full of love and I look to it often for personal support. I'm lucky because it continues in my life today. Understanding its invaluable impact, I pass it along to other children. I always had a moon to guide my path and light my way; it's never wavered and never dimmed.

Villages are important as they make you feel grounded and secure. Without caring adults and meaningful relationships in the lives of children they feel scared and they aren't being taught how to navigate the large and complex world they live in. Children who grow up in multiple families don't develop a sense of belonging and therefore have difficulty understanding themselves, their purpose in life and what special gifts and talents they possess. It should be a primary goal for us to create longstanding connections for children so they can develop to their fullest human potential.

# Attachments and Messages;
# They ALL Matter

*It's what you say and what I hear
that helps define who I am*

One day I had to pick up a young girl and her brother from a foster home where they had been placed for several months. This particular family chose this sibling group to foster because they had met in the community and the mother took a liking to them. This is not an uncommon practice in the world of foster care. Children know they need a family and they canvass their surroundings to find one. As they go through the "courting" stage (found in all relationships), they put on their best "happy face" as they reel you in, because-like all of us-they want commitment and they want connectedness, as was the case for these two children.

Throughout the placement I tried to educate the novice foster parents about foster care and what types of problems these particular children might display while in their home. The children had been seriously neglected at the hands of their birth parents. Neglect rears its ugly head in many ways and for these two it meant little food to eat, unkempt living conditions, poor hygiene and a history of school neglect.

Although I tried to share what I knew about the effects of neglect on child development, the parents disregarded much of what I said; believing love and love alone would right the many wrongs done in the lives of these children. Trauma and vicarious trauma takes a long and hard toll on everyone caught up in the foster care system and its affects transcend from the victim, to the caretaker, and everyone in between. Invariably, the parents eventually grew tired of the ongoing behaviors displayed by the children. As most novice parents remark, the children's behavior was not changing "even though they had lived with the family for several months" and the parents recognized the wrath it was causing with their own children. They reached their emotional and physical limit and requested removal. This was particularly difficult for the little girl because she had grown increasingly attached to this family and more specifically the mother. The young girl never experienced unconditional love from a mother figure and sadly, this too, was being taken away. In her young life she had lived with five or six families by the time she was ten. When this happens, the process of natural attachment to a primary caregiver does not occur. This has longstanding, sometimes irreversible implications. It was somewhat amazing to me this girl had acclimated to this family given all she had endured in her young life. When I picked her up that day, I was devastated by the thought of moving her and no matter how I tried to prepare myself for "the" conversation, I couldn't. It was simply too painful to watch or take part in.

After good-byes and niceties where exchanged, it was time for us to take the car ride to the next family. When I put both children into my car and went to fasten the girl's seatbelt, I noticed she had tears running down her face. I leaned over and asked if she was okay. I told her I knew this was very hard and very sad for her and it was okay to cry if she needed to. She looked at me and said, "I'm not crying, the sun in my face is making my eyes tear." I believe, to this day, this was the very moment in time this child stopped caring about anything. Her life from this point forward went downhill and we couldn't get her back. She wanted to attach and feel part of something greater than herself (as I believe most people do). The disappointment of this opportunity being taken away caused her to stop risking her feelings. The little girl I had known was gone. It was obvious to me "the moon" clearly escaped her grasp, never to shine again. No matter what I said, how I acted or what actions I took, I could not return the moon to her.

Children who don't have a consistent parental caregiver early on in life have difficulty attaching to others throughout their lives. In normal situations children form solid attachments, usually with mothers since they are likely the primary caretaker from birth. Infants, of course, rely on external stimuli to get their needs met. If they cry, the expectation is someone will comfort them, if they are hungry, someone will feed them and when they make eye contact, someone will look back. Sadly enough, many children don't start their lives in this way and as a result, it can be an upward battle trying to trust the environment will respond to their needs. Early attachments are the basic building blocks for future successful relationships and the emptiness left from a lack of attachment is virtually impossible to fill. Children with "holes" have ongoing struggles because they haven't learned how to hold onto what is put into them and adults who try to love these children become frustrated and eventually give up. Relationships are give and take and when you constantly give and receive nothing in return, it's exhausting and devastating.

It's stunning how some people struggle with the simple task of developing lifelong relationships with others. The "collateral damage" of broken early attachments is seen in unfulfilling relationships, latent with hardships, and an ultimate lifetime of emptiness. It's not the fact that some have had these experiences that amazes me; it's the fact an average childhood typically lasts 18 short years; less than a quarter of an average life, yet a lifetime of irreparable damage can occur. The fact some people spend more than three quarters of their life undoing 18 years is an overwhelming reality.

I see adults in my private practice as well as children. One day a 48-year old woman came in. She wanted to understand why her romantic relationships never worked out the way she fantasized they should. Relationships never provided her with what she needed emotionally and only caused her more depression and an increased poor sense of self. Through our work together, we concluded the relationship between her and her father had been strained from childhood into her adult life. She never felt like she made the mark or lived up to his expectations and she wasn't able to recall one happy memory the two of them shared. The negative messages she heard from him as a child became the definition of who she was, and they were always with her. Her father consistently showed disappointment rather than acceptance of who she was and wanted more from her than she felt she could deliver. She couldn't deliver because his expectations were unreasonable, ever changing and unrealistic. Thus, her adult relationships were emotionally draining and she wasn't able to achieve a level of intimacy which felt satisfying or true. One could say she had "attachment" issues. She wasn't confident because early messages taught her she simply wasn't good enough. She never developed a true attachment or trust in others because primary people in her life didn't provide the emotional safety needed. As a result, she held back from her partners because she didn't trust them, and was afraid of their rejection. Once we uncovered the root cause (gave the behavior language she could understand), she was able to begin the change process. Though she was on her way to living a life filled with healthier relationships, the issue was by no means resolved and she continued to run into stumbling blocks along the way. The good news is she was able to recognize them quicker, and able to change how she reacted to them.

Children need to know you are bigger than them, stronger than them and essentially will be their protector and keep them safe from danger. (I think Bill Cosby paraphrased it humorously when he said "I brought you into this world, and I'll take you out!") Whether children consciously understand this or not, they will do everything in their power to get you to stand up and do what you're supposed to as their adult protector. This is the premise behind misbehaving. When children feel unsafe or fearful, they act out. They need to know you will provide boundaries, rules, predictability and safety for them because they don't have the capacity to provide this for themselves. It is frightening when the world (as limited as it may be for them) feels out of control.

I used to repeat this to my nephew, Luke, when he was younger. I'd remind him I was bigger than him, stronger than him and could knock him out if I had to. (I am no longer bigger or stronger than him and he reminds me of this constantly). Though I would say this in jest, I think he understood an adult's job was to protect him. One day while on vacation he and I were in a grocery store. We were being silly and fooling around a little too much. I could see it was getting out of hand so in trying to calm the situation I said, "Luke, wait, I need to say something." He said, "I know, I know. You're bigger than me, stronger than me and you could knock me out!" I wasn't exactly going to use *THAT* one at this time but I laughed because he got the message. He knew we were both getting out of hand and I, as the adult, needed to reel us both in.

Many of the children I have worked with were never given boundaries and thus spent their entire childhood feeling unsafe. If you think about the physiological aspect of this, it means your brain is constantly in unsettled mode and this, ongoing, can be a form of trauma resulting in a true lack of appropriate brain development. This is the child who is more likely hyperactive, easily agitated, and has difficulty regulating his/her mood. More importantly, this is the child who has difficulty calming down or even knowing how to begin to do so.

Self-soothing is a skill we rely on daily whether we recognize it or not. When we are in traffic, we listen to music, when we have trouble falling asleep, we do relaxation techniques-infants innately suck their thumb or rock. Some of what we routinely do is instinctual and some of it is taught from birth by our parents.

I remember working with a sibling group of three-two girls and a boy. Though these three were related, they did not know how to get along with one another. They were never taught the basics of give and take or how to communicate their needs. Additionally, they were almost never in a calm state. They couldn't live together in one foster home because there wasn't a family able to handle all three of them. In fact, it was in their best interest to be placed in three different homes with three different social workers, so each child could receive individualized attention. Our collective task was to help the children develop a sense of self, individuation and basic coping skills with the overarching goal of teaching them how to relate appropriately with one another and with others.

Early on in their lives, this sibling group lived with their birth family members but the home environment was so chaotic and out of control it was difficult to determine who was in charge, what the rules were, if there were rules and where the structure (if any) lay. Neither the children nor the parents knew who was in charge. When the siblings came into care, they didn't possess basic skill sets. They didn't know how to dress themselves, eat with proper utensils or have any knowledge of self-care techniques. They couldn't communicate in an expected give and take reciprocal fashion using age appropriate language. They were essentially feral children who had no individual identity and their primary goal was to get their needs met no matter how; they only knew basic survival. Though they were elementary and middle school ages, they functioned more like toddlers. Their communication style with one another was essentially constant bickering and the bickering almost always ended in full-blown physical aggression toward one another.

The respective foster parents had to teach the children the very basic of basics, and because they were siblings, we felt obligated to teach them how to relate to one another in a civilized manner. I tell this story because this particular sibling group reminds us that, if not taught, children do not innately know how to cope, self sooth or function in what would be considered a normal fashion. They were children who only knew basic survival skills. They literally could not function normally in the world and years of therapeutic work only brought them so far. Their early messages were unintelligible, to say the least, and made no cohesive sense.

Emotionally healthy adults teach their children how to be emotionally healthy adults. They teach them through overt or covert messaging and they do this virtually from day one without even realizing they are doing it. When their baby cries, they pick them up, rock and talk to them in a quiet, calming voice. When their toddler gets out of control, they instruct them to sit down and take a time out. When their seven or eight year old child acts "too big for their britches," the parent responds by saying something to the effect of "you need to stop and think about how you are behaving." These are all good parenting techniques that have a tendency to produce long term, healthy results because they become internalized *coping skills* for the child. Essentially, the parent is teaching the child how to self-assess and providing the tools needed to apply corrective action.

Rocking helps teach an infant that a slow, repetitive action can actually make them feel comforted. It produces a physiological calming response in the body. The toddler learns when they are feeling out of control stopping for a break can help calm them. The seven or eight year old child learns they have crossed the limit and it is time to stop, take a look at what they are doing and change the behavior to something more acceptable.

As adults we use these techniques in everyday life. We draw from what we've been taught. The skills become integrated components of who we are. When my siblings and I were older and out of control, my parents were big on having us stand in the corner until we basically fell asleep on our feet (even though it was likely only five minutes!) We learned when we were ordered to "the corner," it was time to calm down and re-group. They knew they couldn't send us off to bed in a hyper state so they implemented a consequence, which clearly became our "time out" and it taught us something about our own self-regulation.

The absence of well-defined coping and self-soothing skills can cause tremendous anxiety for those who don't have them. This is recognized in the person who is easily shaken, easily frazzled and has difficulty acting quickly on their feet. If you combine this with people who don't possess a solid sense of self, the end result can be toxic because even little things will rattle them to the core and they won't know how to respond appropriately; they don't have the confidence or the skill level to do so.

When a child sits before you, and pierces through the very core of your soul by saying, "I'm not a loveable person," there aren't adequate adjectives to describe how this burns through every part of your being. And if you don't happen to believe what is being said, the child will surely show you by the anger they project, the starvation that hangs from their skeleton and the old and new scars carved deeply into their bodies.

Though I hear these words often by those youth who don't have a true sense of self, I'm still at a loss each and every time these words poison the space in the room. Here is this person tearing themselves wide open and there isn't one thing you can say or do to change their perception of themselves. If you cried, maybe you'd show them true emotion. If you hugged them, maybe you'd show there are people in the world who truly feel compassion. Neither intervention would work well in a moment such as this, especially early on in the therapeutic relationship, so silence permeates like deafening white noise until one of us decides to break it.

I'm intrigued by the fact a person hurts themselves physically and/or emotionally because they believe they should be punished for something, which was never their fault to begin with. Yet the early messages they received were so strong they have convinced themselves their unrealistic cognition is an accurate one. In fact, I don't think I can think of one thing a child can do where this response is warranted. However, we see self-inflicted injury and hear self-deprecating language all of the time. It's out there and despite all of my social work tricks, it's hard to erase old messages in the minds of others. Early messages are embedded into who we are and uncovering the hurt, layer by layer, is the only way to go.

Positive early messaging and strong attachments to others is the key to healthy development. These two concepts pave the way for healthy self-esteem and strong ego development.

Negative and deprecating remarks are like war wounds that rarely heal, despite our greatest attempts. It is considered emotional abuse and should not be overlooked. It causes stagnation in emotional development and is just as devastating as physical abuse, maybe even more so.

# I Like You and You Like Me…
# It's ALL About the Relationship

*At the moment in time when I realize my life would be
empty without you, I know we are connected.*

A preteen began talking after several weeks of
saying little to nothing. Week after week I'd try to
prompt and encourage her. I drew from all I knew, to
no avail. My gallant attempts yielded no noteworthy
results. Grasping for straws, I decided I would simply
be myself and figured she would eventually buy into
the relationship. This would be my ace in the hole.

Instead of her taking the bait, I was met with snide
remarks, testing of my loyalty toward her, comments
about my "only doing this because I get paid to" (I
really would be rich if I could cash in every time this
one was used) and similar remarks skillfully used to
deflect whatever war was going on in her devastated
soul. She was a master at building walls around her.
The only things I knew for sure were she was angry,
sad, broken, scared, confused, distrustful, alone and
lost. She had no sense of self, had no idea how to
develop one and clearly found a way to protect her soul
from the outside world by closing herself off from it.
She admitted to trusting no one and had no interest in
changing this self-defeating attitude. Week after week, I
waited.

The mere fact she broke her vow of silence at all was a breakthrough in and of itself and I marveled in the success of it all. What she confided next was more than I could personally grasp and no professional training could have helped me overcome my own grief upon hearing it. "There is not one person in the world who loves me," she said. I ask, quickly remembering a *"why"* question would put her into defense mode and consequently shut her down, "Okay, how did you reach this conclusion?" She quipped back, "You think you're so smart, you tell me." She begins playing the all too familiar provocative game which she skillfully orchestrates and is the only one who knows the rules. No one else has fair footing because the rules change depending on her call and her mood. She dangles the carrot then quickly takes it back. She continues to test my commitment to her and sits back to watch how I will react. At this point I can tell she wants to trust me but her own experiences of life, love and commitment don't allow her to dive into uncharted waters. She makes a conscious decision not to and pushes away any attempt on my part to get close to her. The confusion whirls around in her mind and I can virtually see her stacking another row of bricks around her body.

I breathe and choose my words carefully because, believe it or not, this is the one chance she is giving me to prove my worth to her. This was one of those rare therapy changing moments where I know I am either part of the problem or part of the solution and since I choose solution, I, in my infinite wisdom respond with the only thing I can think to say, "The only thing I DO know is you are pissed off at something which has happened but I'd be damned if I know what it is." She looks at me, almost with playful eyes and says, "You're an idiot!" Again the exclamation point in my head makes a cameo appearance. I laugh and say, "Thank God we brought that into the open, now I don't have to pretend anymore!" and I smile. Silence deafens us again.

The agonizing, wordless hours, which led us to her next statement, brought it all together for me and finally her life and actions made sense. She discloses her mother, in an uncontrolled rage of anger, told her she should have aborted her when she had the chance. Her mother finishes off by stating she wished she had because she (the daughter) was worthless; everybody knew it and she (the mother) knew it too. Once again, we define ourselves by the early messages we are told about ourselves.

Given the final piece of the puzzle, is it a wonder this girl behaved in unspeakable ways and did profoundly dangerous things to herself-making the average person question her level of sanity? When the whole story is revealed, the behaviors she displays seem more normal than abnormal. She is perfectly sane and trying to make sense of an insane world. How can a mother tell a child something like this? I mean really, what type of a mother says things to their child that has the potential to leave internal scars so deeply cut into their psyche? Even the greatest plastic surgeon wouldn't know where or how to begin the mending process. And speaking of cutting, this young girl did this regularly to release the pain which she could not find words for. I believe her actions to be a metaphoric way to express herself-because she had trouble finding the words to define her pain.

The healing begins. At this point, we are in the infancy stage of our relationship and must continue building. Though this process was painful, it was also beautiful. A child, who trusted no one, took a leap of faith and made a decision to try and trust someone and I was the lucky recipient of her life changing risk. Until now, I couldn't help this girl learn to fight the demons in her mind, nor could I help her to value her own self-worth. Lastly, without this process occurring first, I couldn't begin to help her develop the skills she needed in order to help herself. She missed out on the fundamental skills of childhood and the fundamental building blocks of healthy development; she was therefore unable to build on them. She was clearly moving backwards rather than forward. She needed to keep going back to the moment when her development was interrupted so she could learn how to move forward. When she felt safe, she could progress onward and heal. We were starting from scratch and my job was to help this young lady learn how to use herself as a way to heal her wounds. She needed to become her own best friend. And maybe, just maybe, the moon was still within her reach and we were heading toward it together. And maybe, just maybe, I was the lucky one who could provide her with the corrective nurturing relationship that would free her to catch the moon.

Several years ago I worked with a young boy who lived most of his life in various foster homes, group homes and therapeutic residential facilities. The only true connection he had to his birth family was the relationship he shared with his elderly grandmother. She loved him and he loved her back. Each week I would do the two hour round trip drive so they could visit each other. To me, this was money in the bank. We were building our relationship. The visits helped him to get through the week and I was happy to do it.

When he was younger, he rarely spoke. He'd get into the car, put in his ear buds and fall asleep. Anyone who has a teenager understands adolescents sleep a lot, often and whenever they get the chance. However, sleep can also be seen as a symptom of depression and a coping mechanism to escape the events of real life. It's important to delineate between the two. In this boy's case, sleep was used as a way to numb his never-ending pain.

On those rare occasions when he was freer with conversation, he'd do it non-stop and I used it as a priceless opportunity to learn about who he was and how he perceived his world. Totally coming from a social worker perspective, I'd ask as many questions as I could think of to keep him talking and I made every effort to optimize on those rare teachable moments. I often wondered how much of what I said sunk in. I recognized it wasn't my words which held the value as much as it was keeping him engaged; helping him to understand I was interested and cared about his life and who he was. This was the magic of those moments. It's not uncommon for any of us to feel as though most kids aren't listening when we grace them with our profound words of wisdom. It's not as if they are going to acknowledge to us that something we say is hitting a nerve, (they are far "too cool" for that!) yet we hope and we keep on talking, despite ourselves.

This particular young man could not live with his grandmother because she was older and quite ill. He understood the reasons but yearned to do so nonetheless. This was his family; his one true connection to the earth. She was the one true person who helped him understand his place in the world. His biological mother was not physically, emotionally, developmentally or financially able to provide him with a safe home and instinctively he must have known this-he never asked why he wasn't living with her. He was terribly neglected during his early years; made to exist without food and consistent shelter. The result of this neglect was evident in his delayed emotional, social and educational development. He had his share of limitations and they were obvious.

His adolescence was filled with endless minor conduct issues until the minor altercations snowballed into an assault charge, which landed him in a juvenile detention facility (a prison for youth) for nearly a year. During his incarceration, we stayed connected. I visited him regularly and we talked. We talked about his life, his experiences and how his poor choices got him into an inevitable situation where there weren't enough life-preservers to rescue him from himself. Through conversation, it was clear-he was changing and maturing. He recognized his limitations and was beginning to take responsibility for them. I couldn't have been happier to see his growth and maturity come alive. I felt a sense of sadness a child was developing into a man under the confines of a juvenile delinquency facility rather than in a family setting.

On the day of his release, I went to the store, bought him street clothes to change into and picked him up. As soon as we walked into the parking lot, he knelt down and kissed the pavement. He remarked he never felt as happy as he was at this moment and indicated the sunshine on his face made him realize having freedom meant everything. Taking this opportunity, once again as a teachable moment, I suggested he carve this feeling into his brain so it could be a constant reminder, for every choice he makes from this moment forward has a consequence and a reward. Despite any earlier attempt I had ever made to help him understand this, I recognized his recent experience was certainly a lesson only life could have taught him.

Not long after his release, I had changed positions and hadn't seen him for a while. One day, while working with another agency, I was called down to the lobby because "someone" was there to see me. When I walked downstairs there he was, this young, put together man, dressed in a chef's uniform. I went to him, put my hand on his shoulder and smiled. I was so happy to see his life had turned around. He said to me he had come to show me he had made a good decision, and he wanted me to see how well he was doing. I tried to find the words to express my pride, but I'm not sure I adequately succeeded. He ended our visit by saying he heard many of the things I had said to him during those long car rides, even when it seemed like he wasn't listening. He thanked me for helping and caring about him. This was the last time we ever saw each other.

While reading the newspaper in 2011, I came across an article which explained how he was shot and killed by a relative during a household robbery while his toddler was in the home. The article, as in most cases of journalistic reporting, sensationalized the gruesome details of his murder and focused on the "unsavory" way in which he led his life. I was sad on many levels when I stumbled on the news but felt true pain when I realized no one would ever know how he struggled to survive most of his life. Including his story in this book is my way of paying tribute to how he tried to live life despite the obstacles which were placed before him from the moment he took in his first breath. Though he made his mistakes, he tried the best he could with the limited internal resources he had and was brave enough to develop relationships with others even though his early ones were so damaged. I felt proud to have known him and happy to have been a positive relationship in his life. The moon for him fell dark, and because of the sadness I felt for his tragic end, for me as well.

My definition of the word relationship unknowingly began to take shape the day I was born. It has continued to develop from that point on because my family clearly valued and honored them. Like most families, we fought and we made up. We disagreed and we talked (yelled really; we're Italian!) until the disagreement was resolved. And when one of us felt pain, we rallied to make the person feel better. We had our moments when we needed individual space and when alone time was satisfied, we gathered for family dinners. This was my normal and it was assumed-in my limited view of life at the time-it was everyone else's normal as well.

My parents are emotionally healthy people and they were on a mission to raise emotionally healthy adults. (Well, maybe they weren't *really* on a mission, but they seemed to do it!) This is not to say we didn't all make mistakes along the way, we did and we lived through the discomfort of the mistakes until they were adequately resolved. My point isn't to say I grew up in a perfect family, because I didn't. The point is at the end of each day, we were together and the love and respect we had for one another was evident. We learned how to nurture relationships because little doses were injected into us daily until we got it. It's the day-to-day consistencies of non-wavering messages that teach children; before you know it positive messages become part of their moral fiber and character development. I was lucky. My messages were positive rather than negative, and because of this, personal views of myself were positive.

As I was living my "normal" life, others were not. I had a childhood friend whose family functioned in a polar opposite fashion. Her parents were divorced and didn't get along. They fought every time they saw each other and this poor kid was directly in the middle of their discord. Children of divorce virtually always feel they are partly to blame for the separation and ultimate demise of a family. When there's constant fighting about them in their presence, the unrealistic seed of doubt grows mightier and stronger. This becomes imbedded into a person's self-concept and they walk around with the misperception until they are challenged by it. Their unrealistic cognition becomes their fact.

My friend had parents but the family, by no means, shared relationships with one another. Her parents, based on their own accusatory behavior of one another, certainly weren't teaching her how to have healthy ones. Sure, she was kept safe and fed but her emotional development wasn't nurtured or developed. Nothing was what it seemed and promises were consistently broken. I was the closest thing to a sister she had since she was an only child. She practically lived at our house and my family became her family. It was my parents who taught her the meaning of unconditional love and acceptance. I know this to be true because even when she and I grew up and became more distant, she'd go back to visit them. They were her emotional "home base."

Did my parents know they were providing this for her? Probably not, I think they were just being who they were.

During our adolescent years she struggled to "belong." She had difficulty finding a peer group in which she was comfortable and joined many different groups as a way of developing a sense of self (trying to find her place in the world). It was a long and hard struggle for her to self-identify and given her upbringing, it's not surprising. She didn't receive the proper training or messages early on and spent a number of years attempting to undo the years of damage which plagued her sense of reality and sense of self. Since she was able to find acceptance outside of her family, the moon remained her light. Her personal resiliency enabled her to keep reaching for the moon and to use its light to guide her path; even when darkness prevailed. Her resilience was developed, not by her own parents but rather, by those adults outside of her family who held her close and made her feel special.

I have maintained relationships with many of the kids I've worked with through the years. These relationships have helped them feel valued and led me to become the person I was meant to be. I don't have birth children but have non-biological ones who continue to honor me by staying part of my life. I've watched them grow, struggles and all, into the adults they are today and for this I am grateful. I feel strongly about delivering the message "I care about who they are, what they are made of and what they represent in this life."

When you are trained in the helping profession, you are taught the significance of boundaries. As a guiding force and principle the topic becomes central to the work you do with people and is something you must keep in the forefront of your mind. You learn the importance of boundaries-I respect the general philosophy. However, a good teacher taught me boundaries have a looser meaning than what we were all taught. Boundaries are good, therapeutic and necessary yet they shouldn't be so inflexible whereby they get in the way of the relationship you are trying to build and the corrective experiences you are trying to facilitate. When I went back to "my teacher" years later for further explanation, she simply said, if you choose to stay connected to someone after your professional work is done, ask yourself one question: is the connection for you or for them? When you have answered this question, you will know what to do.

Several years have passed since this lesson was taught and each and every time the opportunity arises, I ask myself the question, which helps me to make the correct decision. Through the years I've determined its meaning to be: If you are there for the overall good of the person and not for your own gratification, then remain as a positive influence within their life. I haven't done this often but I've done it in my career. We are all human and humans need to feel connected. My personal choice to stay involved in a child's life is done primarily for the child/youth because I fundamentally believe relationships are valuable. This is not to say the relationship is without reciprocity, because it most definitely is. Consistency is important and most of the children I have worked with have not had meaningful, longstanding, positive relationships. It's a difficult balance to strike; the act of genuinely offering a part of you while doing the clinical work and then taking it away when the therapeutic work is done. To me, it feels too much like re-traumatizing the child, especially when they have had a lifetime of unhealthy and inconsistent relationships. Where my professional affiliation might not always agree, it's a conscious, well thought out, test of time, choice I've made which has yielded positive results. I have remained involved in whatever capacity fits the need: a friend, a caring adult, a mentor, a support from afar, a cheerleader; and I will continue to do so if the situation calls for it. In the lives of some children, the consistency of a positive relationship is their moon and their light. I'm honored to do it.

Healthy relationships are imperative to our development. Without them, we struggle to gain a sense of belonging. When we feel connected to others, we take the necessary risks to trust and when someone provides us with emotional safety, we learn to love ourselves.

# Foster Care; Are We Helping or Hindering?

F oster care proper is a system set up for children who, for a varied number of reasons, cannot live within their legal, usually birth, families. A number of reasons contribute to the ultimate decision to remove a child from the place they consider home and the decision, no matter how grotesque the circumstances, is never an easy one. Believe it or not, even children who have been horrendously abused rarely want to leave their abusers; especially because the abusers are likely their own parents and despite all things, they love them and these are the people they feel most connected to. When you remove the connection, a child feels lost and abandoned and the emptiness can stay with them forever; leave a hole too great to fill.

Even if children understand, on some level, they are not to blame for the unspeakable things done to them, many still do. They come to this understanding with limited pools of experience and developmental savvy and it's difficult for them to comprehend the complexities of the total picture. It isn't until their brains develop more fully (at the approximate age of 25) when they can begin to comprehend all the nuances involved in the complicated occurrences in their lives. They take from the experience (or experiences) what they take and then try to function in a world which doesn't make sense or meet their needs. In essence, they go into the world with a map and no coordinates so they are already lost.

In reference to brain development, here is a side note: The more we learn, the more we understand the human brain completes its development when a person reaches the approximate age of 25. Because of this, I propose every 25 year old be thrown a "congratulations, your brain is fully developed" party. I think there should be brain shaped cakes, plates, streamers, table clothes, napkins and balloons to fully bring the point home. The guests should all be mandated to wear tee shirts with different brain parts colorfully displayed with each part having a complete description of its particular function. Lastly, I think the honoree should be asked to present a speech on what their brain means to them. Young adults would know we mean business and that all adolescent nonsense (I mean behavior) will no longer be tolerated. Now I've never presented this party idea publicly so if it goes viral, I want full credit for its success and want to be invited to the party!

Though the child welfare system is set up to protect our most vulnerable population, sometimes it feels as though it does more harm than good. We place children in safe places and they run away (from or "to," depending on where they are going). They become angry, empty people with nowhere to turn, no adult to connect with and no moon to light their path. They don't understand why they were removed from their caregivers and they certainly don't understand why they have such limited contact with them. We try to make things as normal as possible for the child but what exactly defines normal in situations like these? If adults can't understand then children certainly don't have the capacity to do so. Foster children have 3$^{rd}$ degree burns to their soul; no one sees them yet foster children feel the raw day after day after day after day. If they are lucky, the pain eventually eases yet more likely, the ache becomes so familiar to them it simply feels normal.

Our child welfare system isn't a perfect one but it's the only one we have and I give credit to those who spend their careers trying to improve and work within it. It's come a long way in my professional lifetime and for this, I am grateful. Right now, with all of its imperfections, we have to find creative ways to work within it, despite its many limitations.

Abuse and neglect are traumatizing and complicated occurrences. Unfortunately, society as a whole has grown numb to what this truly means for those who have experienced it in their lives. The trauma surrounding abusive events, in many cases, leaves more residual damage than the actual act itself. Voluminous amounts of research tell us trauma can actually change the course of normal brain development. The impact of this plays out in how people respond to ongoing life events throughout their lifetime and is why treatment is needed.

Our brain stores information with every experience we encounter and the information spills out when we least expect it. So is the case for traumatic events. Though we might not initially react or understand, the trauma can come out at unanticipated times. This is the case for those who suffer with what has been named "Post Traumatic Stress Disorder." A smell, a color, a noise, can trigger an unexpected response, behavior or reaction. The reactions are just as surprising to the individual person as to those of us who are around when it happens. These are subconscious responses to stimuli stored in the brain and for those who experienced multiple episodes of trauma; it becomes a sad way of life. A more common example would be the Vet who returns from war and has difficulty functioning normally when returned to civilian society. After spending many days, months or years at war, they become accustomed to unsafe and unpredictable situations. Their bodies are always in a "fight or flight" mode; ready to react at the drop of a dime for self-protection. This becomes their normal behavior while in service, so when they come home, their bodies continue to react in the same way when triggered by a stimulus which to others seems mundane. A little noise or a smell can cause them to react in a way, which makes no obvious sense to us. Because we have been home and haven't had the experiences they have had, we can't really understand what is going on with them. Thankfully, there are a number of efficacy based therapy modalities to help deal with the effects of this disorder.

Foster parents and child welfare workers play a role in the healing process for children placed in their charge. It is difficult and grueling work. These two parties are in the forefront; firing line really, helping children overcome years of abuse and trauma. Though we are trained to do so, training alone cannot prepare you for helping children overcome unspeakable sadness and pain. Compassion, humanity and general concern for the well-being of others is equally important.

I hold foster parents in the highest regard. I respect and value them. Without foster parents, this work would be impossible and some children would never be given a second chance at life. These individuals are the ones who are able to hand the moon back to children and give them hope for a happier life. In my career I have worked with the best and some have proven to be my greatest teachers and friends.

Foster parents take on the lion's share of responsibility for healing society's damaged children and this task is a monumental one. The rewards can be great in the long term but in the everyday, it's emotionally draining, tiring and sometimes thankless work. We couldn't possibly repay them for all they do so if you happen to know any, thank them from the bottom of your heart. Neither foster parents nor child welfare staff are adequately paid or praised for the intense work they do. If you take nothing from this book, please take this: ***Caring for abused and neglected children is a 24-hour a day/365 day a year commitment and if the system works as it should, the job extends beyond the child's 18th birthday.*** No amount of money can reimburse this select group of people for the emotional investment they put into the "job." It's done for the love of children, hope for future and an overwhelming attempt to try and right society's wrongs. For most, it's a calling and an honor. Foster parents carry the moon and pass it to children who require light in order to keep on going.

Foster parents subject themselves to anger they did not cause, opposition they did not create and opening of their home to those of us who must come into it on a regular basis. They essentially give up their privacy and learn to accept the fact every move they make will be scrutinized in some way, shape or form. They subject themselves to false allegations made by damaged children who displace their anger and discontent and are judged by others as a result. This is not to say all allegations are false but many are. It's all part of this business.

Once a child becomes a ward of the state, their lives, as well as the lives of the foster parent become open books for all to see. Imagine, for a moment, what this would be like. When perspective foster parents make their interest known, the questions start firing and the endless hours of home study, interviewing and training begins. We examine every aspect of a foster parent's life and assess their motivation to take a child into their home. I'm not saying we shouldn't be this thorough because, after all, we are placing vulnerable children with them; I'm saying I wish all parents had to prove their intentions this well before becoming parents. Could you imagine a world where every person who wanted to have a child needed to pass a test, be fingerprinted, have a lengthy home study written and had to state their intentions as to why they wanted children in their home and be judged on their responses? Any healthy woman can give birth, yet not

48

every person can foster or adopt. It's just one of those things which cause you to go "Hmm" for a moment.

When foster parents enter the system, they do so because they have felt successful in some part of their "child-centered" world and decide they can make a difference by taking another person into their home to love. Where this is a great start, it's only that, a start. Dealing with ongoing behavioral and psychological issues of a broken child takes more than basic love and compassion. It takes training, education and experience because foster children require different parenting than biological children. They need to be spoken to differently, reprimanded and given consequences differently and they need to be loved differently because foster kids are coming into foster families with their own misconstrued, misguided perceptions of how families function, based on their first-hand knowledge. Thus, you can't simply go up to a child with a history of sexual abuse and hug them. A hug has a deeper and different meaning to them. Where our world typically defines a hug as a caring, comforting and nurturing gesture, foster children experience it as another violation of their being and personal space, because other significant adults in their lives have taken advantage of them and touched them in inappropriate ways.

Foster families must be trained prior to receiving their first child, as well as receive ongoing training while the child is in their home in order to maintain their foster care license. Many states mandate a certain number of pre-licensing, post-licensing and yearly training hour requirements. This is to ensure the parents who are fostering have a level of specialized training and expertise in order to parent these very special children who have very special and specific needs.

The intent is good and agencies do their due diligence when preparing foster parents for the journey. However, how do you disseminate information to a group of good-hearted people who really have no idea what they are about to experience? Again, most of us enter new endeavors with preconceived ideas, rooted in our own experiences. It is the social worker's job to help these people broaden their view and accept things which challenge their personal comfort zone and has the potential to rattle them to their core. We must be deliberate in our teachings and everything we do and say must drive the point home. It's an important job because our goal is to create "forever families" or lifetime connections for those children who deserve every bit of that bond.

When I worked for one child welfare agency, several colleagues and I were tasked with creating an orientation for new parents interested in fostering. We knew we couldn't simply get up and speak about all we knew. The special needs of the children we worked with were such a rote part of who we were. Because we understood their needs so well, we had to find creative ways to pass on the information-a way that would be understood and internalized. We needed to be precise in the messages we presented realizing it was imperative people left the experience with a good conceptual framework for what lay ahead of them. Children in our care deserved this and we knew we couldn't afford the mistakes if we didn't do it well. Children's lives were at stake.

In one portion of the training, we drew a little girl on one of those large leaf bags; the ones you use for major yard clean up. At the bottom center we cut a hole, leaving a lip around the edges inside the bag. The presentation consisted of asking participants to look at the girl and decide what positive things they would "give her" if she were a child placed within their home. We had them write all of the things down on a sheet of paper. After they completed the task, we had them fold their papers and come up and place their list into the bag while two trainers held the bag approximately three inches from the ground. The prospective parents had no idea some of the papers they were placing into the bag were falling through the hole on the bottom and were surprised to see this happen. They thought it was an error.

The exercise was meant to show you can give so much of what we believe to be the good stuff to children and still have some of it fall through the bottom (some got caught on the internal lip and remained securely inside). We discussed how this experience helps us to understand, just because we want to pass on good to a child doesn't mean they can or are willing to accept it. It's not a matter of giving up; it's a matter of learning how to "place" the good things so more of them stays inside of the child. This exercise challenges personal parenting techniques and communicates that people take and accept things differently.

51

In another exercise, we handed out nautical maps and wrote nautical coordinates on the board. Without giving any other direction, we asked them to follow the coordinates and tell us where they ended up. Our job was simply to record the comments of the group as they did the exercise and not assist them in any way as they tried to locate the ending point. We heard statements like:

- What is this?
- How are we supposed to do this?
- We don't know how to follow this map.
- Ok, when is this over?
- I don't know where I'm going.
- No one ever taught me how to read a nautical map.
- This isn't fair!

These were perfect, unrehearsed statements that helped parents hone into the foster child's fear about entering a new home with little direction or knowledge about how the home operates or how families operate in general. We made connections by helping them to understand their feelings were shared by the children who entered their home; so they would be aware of where the children were coming from emotionally. We wanted them to feel, on a visceral level, what their foster child might feel. Our goal was to teach using experiential and interactive tools. These are two examples of many used to drive the significant points home.

When I began my career in child welfare, I was given the case of a six-month old baby who was burned on more than half of her body by her father while he was bathing her. When he realized what had happened, he attempted to cut away the dead skin and did not seek medical treatment until several hours later. By the time she was seen by hospital staff, serious infection had set in and the child had emergency surgery to save the damaged skin. Several subsequent surgeries were performed over a period of time in order to graft the skin. Whether the father did this knowingly or not matters less than thinking about the significant consequences and longstanding implications of the abuse itself on this child and her overall development. This child was traumatized by the abuse itself and re-traumatized with each subsequent surgery and further traumatized each time she saw the remaining scars.

The little girl was placed in a foster home; a family who eventually adopted her. This family entered foster care because of the love they had for children and I guarantee you they left the system as completely different people. The care of this child, both physically and emotionally, was a full time commitment. Each family member gave up something of themselves in order to care for her and they did this daily and for years until the physical injuries began to heal. Unfortunately, regardless of what they provided her by way of love, nurturance and physical care, she was not able to overcome her deep-rooted emotional issues; likely caused by the ongoing trauma. If you recall what I said earlier about trauma and brain development, you'll remember that research indicates that incidents such as the one described above can actually arrest or affect brain function and development.

This little girl had physical scars on over 50% of her body which reminded her every day that something went terribly wrong in her life. Since she was preverbal when the abuse occurred, she couldn't tell us what happened but she obviously knew something had. I remember seeing her when she was around seven years old. She didn't remember me specifically but was told I was the social worker who helped her find a home to grow up in. One of the first things she asked me was if I knew she had scars all over her body. When I said I did, she asked me if I knew her father. When I replied that I did, she asked me to tell her everything I knew about him. She was trying to put it all together but struggled to have the story of her life make sense.

The family that took her in was an exceptional family; they loved her and tried to normalize an abnormal situation by providing consistency. I believe the early trauma played a significant role in the outcome of her life and although the moon was placed within her reach, circumstances beyond her control got in the way of her taking full hold of it. Her emotional scars were deep and untouchable and her physical scars were daily reminders someone had damaged her for life. All the training in the world could not have prepared this family for the daily challenges of caring for this girl. I think training helps parents to understand parenting foster children is different but it can never fully teach the indelible impact fostering will have on their own personal growth and life path.

Although some children have constant reminders of their abuse as indicated by the physical anomalies left behind, they also live with the scars not seen by the human eye. This poses an unfortunate disability for them because they "look" normal and thus are treated as such by all who see them. It's hard to imagine something can be "wrong" with someone who looks perfectly normal. However, if you were to tear them open, the scars would be raw, evident and blinding. We, those in the helping profession, engage in ongoing education so we can teach the needs of these damaged children to foster parents on a regular basis.

What some see as failure, I see as success because any intervention provided increases the contents of a person's "tool box." Regardless of the immediate outcome, I believe a child is better off because he/she was given another chance. One has to hope an intervention executed along the way will produce an impact somewhere down the line. Sometimes we are fortunate enough to see the impact and sometimes not. In my life I've experienced both. When kids grow up and come back they tell you what was helpful and what was not-you learn for the next time. The feedback has been an invaluable teaching tool for my development as a social worker and clinician. I look back now and wonder how many things I have said which were insensitive or thoughtless just because I didn't know any better. As the old saying goes, "You don't know what you don't know," until someone tells you or you figure out your deficiencies on your own. Thank goodness children allow you numerous chances.

Foster care is set up to protect, but it has no way of preventing and this is the issue. When you're coming into the game after it has already started and without the proper equipment for a strong defense, you don't get much of an opportunity to impact the final score. By the time damage has been done, it's hard to backtrack, yet we try. We try because most of us believe hope and resiliency will prevail. If we didn't support this basic tenet of the field then we wouldn't find the courage to keep going. People who are willing to explore unchartered waters with others are brave individuals and it's this bravery that helps to guide the journey.

Though the push for many states, Connecticut included, is to find a family for every child who needs one, sadly it might not always be possible, given a child's specific need. For this reason, there needs to be treatment options available, as one size rarely fits all. There are times when the intimacy of family life is too much for a child who has trouble attaching to others. In circumstances such as these, it's helpful to have other plans available. This is not to say I believe children shouldn't have a family resource (regardless of whether or not they live full time with them) because I strongly believe they should. Families heal. In my mind there is no question. What I am saying is sometimes a child will function better if they can share their loyalties with a number of significant adults. This is what you would find in a congregate care setting.

Congregate care is typically a group home (a place where children live under 24-hour adult supervision) or a therapeutic residential placement center (24-hour care which includes therapeutic intervention to help children overcome emotional trauma and behavioral issues). In these facilities the child feels less pressure to connect. The expectation for intimacy or true attachment to a parent or family member is significantly reduced.

There are "pros and cons" to such a living arrangement. The "pros" are listed above. The "cons" are congregate living facilities contain children with poor behavior, a limited understanding of boundaries, an inability to attach and more. This has a tendency to spread like wild fire and it impacts peer socialization and emotional development of the group. We find most success in using these facilities when there is a family waiting in the wings; ready and prepared for the child's return. Return to a family system, hopefully the birth family, should be our primary goal. The family must be well versed and well trained in the child's specific issues.

Another negative outcome results when a child remains too long in a congregate care setting. They become too comfortable within the facility and helping them move into a family environment is difficult, if not impossible. The reasons how/why this happens are far too great to mention here but one of the main reasons is the child may experience a fear of failure. Again, their past experiences dictate their belief about what family living can mean and they are frightened. The feeling might be best described by considering the following: How many times would you walk to the altar if in the past your partner was not there waiting there for you? You might do this one other time, maybe two but you'd likely not do it a third time. The same is true for children whose family experiences have not been positive.

While working in a residential facility, the staff experienced this with a teenage boy who we tried to return to his biological family. Though returning home was not seen as the optimum plan, the youth was an older teenager, returning home was seen as the best possible plan for success. Each and every time a return was scheduled, he behaved in ways which failed to warrant his discharge back to community living. Each time we attempted, he raised the ante until his escalating unsafe behaviors landed him in another highly specialized and restricted facility better prepared to deal with his issues.

This young man obviously couldn't find the words to tell us he was scared and did what he knew best, he showed us through behavior. We clearly misread the signs he was giving. Hindsight is another marvelous trick of the brain. It's possible he knew he couldn't do what we were asking of him and even though there were system mandates that wanted him home, we shouldn't have made a plan this youth didn't approve of. He was scared and needed more time. We shouldn't have rushed the process. We should have stopped, listened and planned accordingly to meet his need. Fortunately, I learned a valuable lesson about what not to do moving forward in my practice. I will do everything in my advocacy role for children to not let something like this happen again. I believe our lack of awareness of his needs caused him additional unnecessary anxiety and prolonged his recovery.

Again, every attempt should be made to find a family for every child but we can't get caught up in the goal of putting square pegs in round holes. We should do what is in the best interest of the individual child/youth. If a child isn't able or ready to live in a family full time then a visiting family should be found so the child is able to call someplace home, have a place to go on holidays, school vacations and into adulthood. A long term goal of permanent residence within a family setting should remain our focus.

Not all children who are abused and neglected end up in foster care even though it seems they should. Somehow they manage to slip through the cracks. This happens often, especially with older youth. It happens with younger children whose neglect or abuse experience isn't deemed "bad enough for removal" by child welfare investigators and the juvenile court system. This is not a criticism because removal of children has to follow the letter of the law and should only be done when absolutely necessary. I'm only suggesting it's sad for those who have fallen through the cracks and have been left behind to grow up in circumstances which don't embrace their full growth potential.

Michelle and I met when I was working in a child guidance clinic in a neighborhood health clinic. Although I wasn't responsible for her care, we'd see each other often when she came in. As our relationship developed, I learned significant details about her life as a teenager growing up in a low-income neighborhood with a mother who was actively using drugs and rarely home. By no means did her mother deserve this title, according to my definition, she wasn't acting like one. Though I understand her biological mother was living out her own lifetime dysfunction, the titles of mother and father are something that should be earned and not taken for granted. Many believe just because they gave birth, the title is automatically theirs. I don't agree though I must say this has challenged my internal value system.

Michelle's mother would leave her children alone for days at a time with no food and no electricity, in a neighborhood which was frightening during the day, let alone at night. The doors and windows were broken and there was essentially no protection from the fear of night. She, her brother and sister were vulnerable in a parentless household and she was scared every day of her life.

Often times Michelle would call me in the middle of the night saying she was there alone and was afraid. Her brother and sister often found their own places to go so they didn't have to be there. As I mentioned earlier, it's not uncommon for kids to find their own resources when their families are not available and are non-functional. It's a fundamental desire to want safety and predictability in life; let alone food, water and a clean place to shower and sleep.

I would get in my car after getting the early morning calls for help and bring her to my house so she would have all of the things she needed. This went on for weeks until I notified the state child welfare agency of my concerns. Michelle and I were basically told her current age (she was an almost 18 year old high school senior trying, despite all odds, to finish her senior year so she could move onto college) prevented her from entering the foster care system.

Since I couldn't, under good consciousness, let Michelle live under those conditions and because Michelle didn't want to, she moved into my house until she finished high school. Her high school graduation was probably one of the sweetest I've ever attended as I knew the struggle it took for her to reach this milestone.

After high school, Michelle went to College earning a bachelor's degree and then her master's degree in Social Work (imagine that!); all the while staying physically and emotionally connected to me. As she got older, she developed her own support network of professional affiliates who helped create the compassionate, giving person she is today. Her specialty is working with abused and neglected children; she worked in a child welfare agency for many years. It doesn't take a rocket scientist to figure out she chose this path as a way to close the gap and understand her own childhood story. She needed to find a way to understand her own journey and perhaps do some good for other children who shared her experiences.

Michelle was "too old" to enter the child welfare system but worked feverishly to try and find her own safe place and to complete her goals. No man is an island and she instinctively knew she needed adult supervision and guidance. She wasn't getting it from her own mother so she found other mothers who could fit the bill. Lucky for me, I was one of the people she chose to help her succeed and through this experience, I was given the opportunity to grow and learn as well.

Much of this work is about teaching others how to be self-sufficient. Michelle gave me the opportunity to teach her how to be a moon for others. She was a good student. She took the lessons she learned and passed them on to others. It's a clear example of paying it forward and I feel proud of the woman she became.

Foster care is not a perfect system. It probably never will be. The responsibilities connected to the system mandates are too great and too overwhelming. As I said earlier, it's the only system we have and we have to work within the guidelines of it. Surprisingly enough, we continue to do exceptional work, despite the limitations, and many children have found their moon in the support and love of many caring adults and families. In time, most children find their way and make sense of the chaos which defines their lives. In time, healthy relationships and experiences and proper services, children are able to connect the dots and find the pieces of their life puzzle-they can understand how they got from point A to point B.

For those of us in this field, we continue to strive towards the development of a better system; a system which truly meets the needs of vulnerable children. We know much more today about child development and the effects of trauma on human development. This knowledge helps stakeholders and politicians to understand too.

Without a comprehensive understanding of the effects of trauma on development, legislation would not be written to significantly impact mental health and child welfare law and policy. Social workers have been an integral part of this progression and will continue to be as the profession continues its growth and notoriety in the eyes of the public.

Unfortunately, foster care is necessary in our society. Children who cannot live with their biological families require a nurturing environment in order to grow into healthy adults. Nationally, the "system" is not perfect but those of us in the field tirelessly work to improve it because we value its mission and purpose.

Children belong in families as this is where healing begins. Even in those cases where children need residential care, the care should be short lived, goal oriented, and a family resource immediately identified. Biological families should not be overlooked as viable resources when it comes to long term planning.

Foster families help provide vulnerable children with what they need and try to right the wrongs done at the hands of their abusers. Though abusers are perceived by society as vicious people, I have come to learn they do the best they can, given their own limitations and life stories. We need to help these individuals as much as we need to help the children who have fallen victim to them if the cycle is to end.

# The Many Sides of Adoption

F amilies are created in many ways and adoption is certainly one of them. Children are adopted at all ages and with every age, there are developmental milestones that must be recognized and addressed. Adoption should never be a secret and every child, despite their chronological age, should be told how they entered their current family. Nothing is more traumatizing for a child than finding this information out unexpectedly or later on in life.

When I was younger, as is consistent with older siblings, I was teased tirelessly by my brother and sister. One "teasing moment" remains clear in my mind as it was the moment they both told me I was "the only one of the three of us who was adopted." They carried this on for what seemed to be hours but I'm sure was only minutes before my mother stepped in to shut them down. What I remember most from this experience was feeling very sad because I felt like I didn't belong and I wasn't really one of them. I was only a child, but I remember this feeling clearly. I don't know if I thought this was a particularly bad thing, I just remember distinctly feeling like an outsider and it didn't feel good to me.

Despite our experiences or how we entered families, we all need to feel like we belong there as part of a greater whole. I'm a strong adoption advocate because I firmly believe every child should have a family and roots from which to build a life and lasting relationships, despite how the family was created.

Adolescence is a particularly "thoughtful" time for all children. This is the developmental period when kids are trying to determine who they are, who they look like, where they got the color of their hair and eyes, sense of humor and so on. Genetically passed-through characteristics are things biological children take for granted because as they grow up, they can see with their own eyes, which family member they resemble; and have heard with their own ears, stories about family and relatives along the way. By adolescence, they've been told a hundred times how much they look like their mother, father, siblings or great aunt so and so.

Adopted children, unlike birth children, do not have this vantage point from which to draw. They know they don't look like the family they are living with and this can cause confusion and uncertainty. This is why gathering as much information about biological family pre-adoption is a gift for children. It's a history held and passed on. This includes all physical and mental health issues. Pictures of biological family members are also a great gift because photos of an adopted child's biological family are priceless puzzle pieces as they attempt to create their physical and personal identity.

There are many players in the adoption arena and each deserves a star role for the parts they play. There are the biological parents/family, adoptive parents/family and, of course, the adopted child who straddles both worlds. Though the child has been legally freed for adoption and subsequently adopted, he/she spends a good portion of their life wondering about birth family. This is a normal and expected part of the adoption trajectory. In a sense, there is a huge piece of his/her life which remains unknown and most use a lot of brain space trying to find the missing pieces. There is a story that has not been told. The adopted child is left to wonder or make up their own story to satisfy the void. I am reminded of a scene from the musical "Annie" where she glamorizes why her birth parents left her in an orphanage. Come to find out, the reality of Annie's life is nothing as she thought. When kids don't have the full story, they need to make one up in order to satisfy the emptiness and hurt left behind. It's a way to cope with the unexplainable and a way to complete their circle so they can carry on.

Many adopted children feel either an overt or covert sense of abandonment. The abandonment translates into an insatiable emptiness and loneliness. Without proper therapeutic intervention or honest conversation this can cause unresolved issues which are carried long into adulthood. I am not suggesting children learn the often times gruesome details of how they came into care. What I am implying is children should be told in age appropriate ways with tempered information. This has to be honest but cushioned and customized to the current developmental stage of the particular child. The last thing wanted is for children to feel as though it's their fault they were given up for adoption. Many already feel this way and even though it clearly isn't their fault, it's an innate and universal feeling for most. Let me also mention here girls and boys typically seek out and process their adoption information differently. Girls, based on their limited perspective and limited ability to understand, tend to internalize the reasons rather than understand there are many reasons why birth parents give up their children or have them legally taken from them. Boys are typically more "matter of fact" about it.

Recently working with a young lady in my current position, I was part of a family meeting skillfully orchestrated by the girl's clinician. The girl asked her clinician to gather her birth parents together for a family meeting. Unbeknownst to me, this was the first time the parents were able to sit in the same room together. They managed to do this without arguing with one another; both things were a first.

This girl asked for the opportunity to sit with her parents and ask them questions for which she needed answers. These were longstanding questions for which only her parents would have answers. She needed to understand the primary reasons why she wasn't living with either of them. She did this because she needed to complete the circle and gaps in her life. She did this in order to begin her own personal healing process. The fact her parents even showed up was a gift beyond gifts. I felt an enormous amount of respect and was awe-struck by them and this young lady for having the courage to participate in the meeting. She fired very difficult questions at them and they tried, as best they could, to remain calm as they helped her to understand why she wasn't with them; why they couldn't get along; how and why she was sexually abused and unprotected from her abuser and how/why they began using drugs. What she wanted most from this meeting was an apology from them-she got what she yearned for. In all of the turmoil of this girl's life, she had the wherewithal to understand she couldn't move on unless her parents were able to move outside of themselves and help her to understand how her life spun so terribly out of her control.

The above was a true therapeutic intervention. She needed real answers to real questions. Without having the ability to look into the future, I can say with certainty this child will never be the same person having had this conversation with her parents. I don't know where life will lead her but I do know she will travel with a more complete understanding of her life history. If she doesn't draw from and make better immediate life choices as a result of this conversation, I have to believe once full maturity kicks in, she will value the opportunity she received that day in a cold, windowless room. Her moon, handed to her by her parents, will not fall far from her sight.

### *The adopted child*

My young friend "K" has a significant trauma, abuse and neglect history. Regardless of the fact she was adopted into a marvelous and compassionate family at the age of seven, her struggles, low self-esteem, poor choices and overall reduced sense of self continues to worsen years into what many would constitute as a consistent and loving home. "K" not only remembers much of her early years, she has been given additional age appropriate information throughout the years to help her fill in the gaps of her memory. This was done in a strategic and planned manner in order to help her cope with all she endured as an infant, toddler and latency age girl. Her story has not been an easy one to tell but one which had to be told in order to help her understand her behaviors and family relationship avoidance. This is a child who, despite the fact she spent half of her life in a stable and emotionally healthy family, has had difficulty fully acclimating. In her case, it's not only the early trauma and multiple moves which have caused great pain, but there is a history of mental health issues which were genetically passed on and contribute to her difficulties. She has attachment issues and has had a significant trauma history. She suffers from post adoption peer related trauma which is preventing her from moving forward. Thankfully, her parents are well-educated and committed people who are in it for the long haul. They came into the adoption world because they had love to give and have grown into people they probably didn't imagine they were when they began this journey with her. All of the education in the world could not have prepared them for the experience of parenting a non-related child with a significant history; they feel more evolved because of the experience. Though "K's" saga continues and her troubles are not behind her, she has made strides within this home which she would have never made if not given the chance and important information. This is a youth who will likely struggle for a good portion of her life because there are many pieces of her life which she needs to understand. Her parents hold the moon in their hands and she will fully take hold of it when she is emotionally capable and physically strong enough to do so.

One day, while in a therapy session with an adolescent girl who spent many of her early years in an orphanage prior to being adopted, it became increasingly clear she didn't understand, with any clarity, where she came from. She insisted the unknowns were not important to her, although I didn't really believe this. She displayed many of the symptoms of a child who had difficulty attaching to adults. She was adopted by a perfectly lovely family and despite the mother's attempt to get to know her; the adolescent was distant and basically non-communicative. She rarely identified her feelings and expressed them even less. It was difficult to engage her in our sessions because she kept total control over what was and was not discussed. This is not to say we didn't have a relationship, because we did. This is to say the relationship was superficial and fairly one-sided at best.

In my experience children who have had rocky beginnings do not have a sense of who they are. They don't know and therefore can't identify a vast array of feelings. They don't know how to read their bodies and consequently cannot tell you how they are feeling about anything. It seems they live life from afar and feelings, to them, are like a foreign language, asking about them results in a puzzled look. Within the therapeutic setting, you have to teach this child how to identify and label feelings, as well as understand how their bodies react to them.

One day, and much to my surprise, she walked in and brought with her a journal. I asked her if she had been doing homework prior to coming because I was curious as to why she had it. "No. I wasn't doing homework." So I dropped it. She's very good at the cat and mouse game so I strategically made a choice not to play this game with her (curious as to where she would take the conversation). A few minutes later she said, "This is the book I write in." Oh, I said. That's nice. Do you want to play a game with me today? She replies "nope" in her general "give me a break" tone so I waited. In a moment she said, "I write poems in this book." I knew she was baiting me but I figured I would give this a little more time so I said, "Oh, that's nice." This was killing her because she wanted me to ask her questions like I normally do, but I didn't. I was being strategic. I thought if I jumped on this opportunity she would pull back and I wouldn't get her to talk at all. Finally, she blurted out, "Do you want to hear them or don't you?" I answered with "Of course I want to hear poems you wrote! Lay them on me!" (Welcome back exclamation point in my head!)

She proceeded to read the most beautiful, well written, and well-thought out pieces of poetry I've ever heard. They were fantastic and insightful and I told her so. She doesn't take compliments well so she basically brushed them off as a non-significant editorial from someone she thought was less than cool. She then suggested something which was completely out of character and asked if we could both write poems today. My head was screaming with excitement but I wasn't going to let her know this. I wanted her to have all the control she needed; I knew this was the only way to go with her. We were really getting somewhere on this day and even though she probably didn't think so, I did. This was my chance to go places with her she never let us go before, so I eagerly agreed as I already knew whatever I wrote was going to be written about her. We each took a couple of minutes to write before she asked if we could read them aloud. My first poem, which she totally got, was this:

## __This Girl__

I sit with this girl,
very pretty (I might add),
week after week.
You would think,
after all of this time,
I'd know who she is;
what she thinks about,
what makes her sad,
what makes her smile-
But I don't.
Silence fills the air.
I can tell, because I can see
by her actions,
that she's kind and smart,
and that she builds tall, sturdy walls
to keep her safe;
to stop the hurt

she must feel.
One day,
probably in the not so distant future,
her walls will collapse
and she'll let another person in
to keep her company.
She won't feel scared and alone anymore!

I kept looking at her while reading and I could see she was smiling and interested. I asked her if she knew whom I was writing about and she said she did but didn't say much more. It was enough for me to know she let me say all of this to her without interrupting. She set up a non-conventional scenario where it was clearly easier for her to communicate-miraculously, and was not emotionally threatening to her. She read her poem which she felt was not one of her best and wanted to continue. She asked if there was enough time for us to write another one. Of course I agreed and would have made more time because I knew she was giving me the opportunity of a lifetime here. My second poem read:

### **The Orphanage**

Living in an Orphanage
among the masses
must be lonely.
There are so many "other" kids
and no one is there to make you feel
special and unique.
So many other children crying,
reaching, demanding attention.

It's so annoying and I get lost
in the crowd.
No one sees me.
Sure, I get fed-
but I don't get nurtured.
I get held-
but I don't get any love.
This is my life.
Then one day,
a person comes to claim ME
and makes me THEIRS.
I am held,
I am loved,
I am special (to someone)
I am me.
I finally get to live!

When I was finished reading, she laughed and asked me why my poems were so good. I joined her laughter and said because they were about her! She told me she knew this and smiled. I folded up the pieces of paper and told her they were a present for her to keep. She took them and left.

This session was a simple, yet meaningful exchange. It remains to be seen but I think this made our relationship take a turn for the better. Though her poems were well written and telling, I'm not sure she personally connected to the words she wrote because when I tried to make the connection for her; she disagreed and gave me "the look" which clearly meant I needed to drop it.

Many adopted children, like the one above, have had many life-altering experiences before they were even able to speak. They've had to interpret things, like the meaning of relationships, based only on guttural instinct and feeling rather than by example. Imagine being one of many, all living in a congregate care environment and not being special to any one person. Your cries are blended into the masses to the point where no one recognizes you are even crying. Since an infant's mode of communication is done largely through crying and babbling, this means they are talking and no one is listening. If you lived enough days under these circumstances, you would quickly begin to believe the world does not pay attention to you when you speak and you learn to rely only on yourself. It's a hard habit to grow out of just because you (all of a sudden) are adopted by a family who wants to pay attention and listen-a family who wants to hand you the moon. This is the exact scenario that creates children who have difficulty attaching to others.

I am known professionally for my work with adopted children. Adoption is a particular interest of mine and I get excited when work with a new child begins. In collecting information from parents and children in order to begin, I typically see the parents and child together for the first meeting so we are all clear about our therapeutic goals. A routine question I ask parents is, "How much brain space do you think thoughts of adoption take up in your child's head?" Where most adoptive parents realize the importance of openly discussing adoption with their child and are proud of their recognition, they almost always answer the question vastly differently from their child (who I also ask in front of the parents). When parents hear how their child responds to the same question, their faces show extreme surprise! The truth is most kids tell me thoughts of adoption take up approximately 80-90% of the space in their heads while adoptive parents typically say 10-20%. This difference in perception is significant and suggests we must close the gap so all parties are operating from the same starting point.

### *The Birth Mother*

When I was in high school, a very good friend became pregnant. Like most teenagers, she had limited choices as to what to do. Her family rallied together and immediately sought counsel at an adoption agency. She was urged to give the child up for adoption. Confused and scared, she thought about it throughout her pregnancy. Ultimately feeling that there was no positive support system for keeping the child, she opted for adoption. This was not what my friend wanted and she lamented about it.

Within her first trimester, she learned she was having twins and thus began mourning the loss of two souls rather than one. As her belly grew bigger, so did her sadness. I'm not sure if having two children over one made this process harder for her but I do know that it complicated her grief; a grief she couldn't share with the people who were supposed to be the closest to her-her family. She felt she had no choice but to give her children up for adoption as talk of any other option was non-existent. This created feelings of loneliness, helplessness and a lack of resolve which continues today.

My friend, a teenager and unwed mother was pregnant over 30 years ago and at the time if you weren't married there were few reasonable choices: Abortion or adoption. Since she was born into a devout Catholic family, abortion was unheard of. However, the most obvious choice for her, keeping and raising her children was not even discussed. No one spoke about the fact that this was new life that needed to be celebrated.

Each and every day of this woman's life, like many mothers who have given children up for adoption, she thinks about her boys. Her mind continuously travels back to the day in the hospital when everything went dark; the exact moment a part of her life slipped quickly and quietly away from her grasp. Metaphorically speaking, there was a death with no funeral. She never had closure or forgiveness. No one sent flowers and no one talked about the fact that someone had "died." She struggles each and every day and longs to see her children today-even for a moment. Like the adopted child, the birth mother yearns for the "rest of the story." She needs to know her children are okay, safe, loved and have turned into whole adults. Many adopted children yearn to have "the conversation" with their birth mother to learn, once and for all, why they were given up; some birth mothers wish for the same opportunity. Without this knowledge, neither will ever feel complete and the moon won't glow its bright light in their world.

Adoption laws are meant to protect all those involved. If a mother goes searching for the child she gave up for adoption, identifying information is not given. If a child seeks information, he/she is given what has been left for them by the birth mother.

Both children and adoptive parents are protected by privacy laws. Though this makes every bit of sense, it doesn't make life easier for people who can't get beyond the grief they feel. In the case of my friend, the only thing she can do is keep her identifying information updated in the boys sealed record so if they happen to go searching for her, they know where to find her. She updated her file five years ago when she and I went back to the agency that handled the adoption. Though we could not legally be given any information and the boys' identity was held in the highest secrecy, the agency staff helping us had the information at her fingertips. She knew all but was unable to share any of it. It was heartbreaking. It's a waiting game and the only way progress will be made is if the boys begin to search. Again, boys process their adoption differently than girls do and usually search, if they search at all, at a much older age and usually after they marry and begin having children of their own. To date, her children have not searched for any information and until my friend is able to close this chapter of her life, it will continue as an oozing, open wound that refuses to heal.

Many birth mothers live with unspeakable grief and loss throughout their lifetime. A piece of them is missing and can't be filled until they meet the child they gave birth to. No one wants to talk about it because the idea is if we don't mention it then it didn't really happen, so imagine the loneliness which prevails within their lives. If you don't talk with adopted children about their loss, it feels to them like the subject is bad or taboo. The same holds true for the woman who gave up their child. Lastly, it's also true for the woman who is unable to give birth due to infertility. The losses, from many perspectives and aspects, are part of the lives of all involved and must be discussed in order for healing to occur. I know this to be true having worked with all the players in the adoption world.

## *The Adoptive Parent*

Parents who decide to adopt have done so, hopefully, after much thought, consideration and training. Some adoptions are costly, especially those done internationally, so it also entails a large financial commitment. There is significant soul-searching which has likely occurred because the decision to expand one's family should not be done nonchalantly. It's not always easy raising a child who is not biologically yours because you not only live with the child; you live with the ghosts which are an integral part of the child's life story. In my opinion, the best adoptions are those where the biological family and adoptive family have a relationship with one another, known as an open adoption. This expanded relationship helps the child develop a full sense of who they are. The latter should only be done if the birth parents are emotionally capable of such a commitment and don't cause interference but rather support to the new family system.

Those who choose adoption often come to this decision due to infertility issues within the family. Infertility represents the loss of a dream or longstanding fantasy and this loss needs to be fully addressed prior to adoption proceedings. If not, one might set up a subconscious dynamic where too many unrealistic expectations are placed on the adopted child. This could set the child up for failure because he/she would never be able to meet the expectations of someone's fantasy.

Adoption is not always an easy road. There is much you don't know when you choose to parent an unrelated child. There's an entire history you might not know and this history can play out for a lifetime. This is even so with infant adoptions because infants have had a gestational period; a period of development, which charts the course for future development.

Several years ago, while working in my state's child welfare department, I was talking with a co-worker about a case I had where a young girl became pregnant. While relaying the fact the girl was only 13, my colleague responded, "OH MY GOSH, I thought boys shot blanks at that age!" Well, they don't. Young boys; children themselves, actually become fathers and young girls; whose emotional and physical bodies are nowhere near ready, become mothers. It was clear to me adoption was the best alternative for this young mother because there wasn't going to be any family support to help her, yet it wasn't my role to make the decision. She had rights, however, she was not convinced adoption was the best choice, and much work needed to be done in order to help her reach a decision which made sense for her and her baby. I met with her day and night during her last trimester to no avail. It wasn't until the 11th hour that she reached her decision. Within hours after giving birth, she voluntarily signed over her parental rights of her newborn baby boy. I brought her the papers while she was still recuperating from a cesarean. I took the baby from the hospital and placed him with a family who had been waiting for an infant for many years.

The benefit to this adoptive family and child was I had the case from day one. I was with the girl and her extended family and was in the hospital throughout the birth. I carried information of this child's life and was able to pass it on to the new family. Little was left for interpretation. I had information on the birth family and genetic history; the adoptive family received it all. For the adoptive family, it was as close to giving birth as humanly possible. This child came with history and the information needed to help complete him. In addition, and kudos to his birth family, we were able to give him several photographs and family stories.

In the world of adoption, this is not always the case and many children come into the "system" without the information they need in order to feel complete. As social workers, we are left to paste the pieces of the picture together with limited supplies. Our finished product is not the greatest work of art. There are holes, rips and gaps in the finished product. The aesthetic value is less than pleasing to the eye. For those of us left caring for children who don't feel complete; parents, siblings, social workers, and teachers it is a daunting task to "create a story" which can answer the unanswered questions. We do the best we can because we understand the importance of the moon and we want to pass on the light.

Through adoption, families are created. Social workers and those involved in the adoption process have the awesome task of providing as much information as possible to the adopted child and parents in order to fill the gaps of the child's life; complete the unfinished story.

Adoption involves many players and each player should be treated with compassion and care. Each has experienced a significant loss that likely leaves an internal emptiness difficult to fill. Many spend a good portion of their life attempting to fill in the missing pieces and heal from the open wounds.

# My Moon

*If we use light to guide us,
the dark of night is more inviting*

For many years, I found myself perplexed by life's uncertainties, the lack of fairness in the world and the struggles which are so clearly present in people's lives. I wanted answers to the big questions but never got them in a way I understood or that felt satiating to me. In hindsight, answers were probably always there but I didn't know how to interpret them. My faith had been challenged and my beliefs on various issues had been rattled to their core. I could not help it. I am generally a positive person but sometimes a positive outlook fails to make realistic situations easier to handle or understand. Ultimately, I could not understand why my life was so good while others suffered routinely. There were people who were hungry, frightened and alone, while I was living a life where these stressors never entered my mind. I had a childhood filled with love and opportunity while others struggled to pay their next bill and find their next meal. I had parents who loved me while others struggled to find a parent to love. My moon consistently provided light, while others struggled to find the light. Nothing made sense. It took many years of pondering and soul searching. When I finally allowed a stronger connection to (and a deeper understanding of) my personal belief in a higher power,

I no longer felt confused by the unjust. I have been building upon my spirituality ever since.

In my opinion the greatest part of human spirit is it refuses to give into life's challenges. I've witnessed this time and time again with those I've met. It's like there's a fire that keeps burning and when life gets rough, the fire dims but never fully extinguishes. I have come to define this slow burn as resiliency; the moon. Although I don't fully understand what level of resiliency a person enters into the world with and how they develop what they have throughout the years, I have come to believe it is their life experiences coupled with caring adults who refuse to give up on them. This dictates how much faith they have in something better crossing their path. I've also come to learn people make choices for themselves despite their histories, and most navigate their own ship.

While working in a homeless shelter, there was an older man who lived on the streets. Because it was our business to find the homeless a place to call home, we worked on this guy, almost daily, until he finally agreed to enter the shelter. We'd offer him coffee, a hot shower, a meal but he always graciously declined our hospitality. This went on for over a year. One day, however, when we offered (what we believed to be inviting) shelter, he agreed.

We were very excited and felt it was a feather in our cap. We were doing our due diligence as professionals and finally intrigued him enough to come in for help. Our consistency and outreach proved successful.

The afternoon he came in, I had one of the male staff take him to the showers; my job was to go buy him a new outfit as the one he was wearing was old, torn, too small for his large stature and hadn't been laundered. Just as I was walking out the door, the staff member came to me and basically said, "Houston, we have a problem. I can't get his socks off." I asked for further explanation and he told me the gentleman's socks were literally stuck to his legs. Though it was a male shower, I was going in. I couldn't believe what I was hearing. My staff member appeared shaken by what he witnessed.

I entered the shower area to see the homeless man sitting hunched over the bench cradling his head in his cupped hands. I walked over and put my hand on his shoulder. I couldn't help but wonder if he thought he had made an error in judgment by coming in. I knelt down to see what the problem was and quickly realized the staff member was accurate in his explanation. This man had urinated on himself so often his socks practically melted like a net onto his bare skin and the frigid weather closed the deal. His socks were not coming off without help. When I asked the man the last time he showered, he told me he had taken one earlier in the day. I didn't want to embarrass him but I said "You and I both know you didn't shower today," though he was persistent in his answer. I didn't press him because this exchange was not about a power struggle but rather an opportunity to give this man his dignity.

I asked the staff member to get me some warm water and a cloth so I could peel the fabric off. As I gently washed away the sock from each leg and foot, the man quietly whimpered and began to tell me how his ankles had been sore for a long time and he hadn't received medical treatment because he didn't know where to go for it. I assured him his medical needs could be met within the shelter and I thought it was a good idea for him to stay and get checked out by a medical provider. As I cleaned away enough of the sock to see his skin, I could see gangrene had developed on most of his leg. I thought to myself this is no way for a person to live. Though this was one of the most humbling things I think I've ever done in my life, I tried not to let my discomfort of the situation show. The man had a right to be treated with compassion.

We finally got him into the shower, taught him how to use soap and shampoo and how to brush what was left of his rotting teeth. I went to the store to buy him clothes, under garments and shoes, my original task. All the while I'm shaking my head and wondering how this happens in a wealthy area like Fairfield County, Connecticut.

Some people choose their life's course, as was the case of our friend. He stayed long enough for us to find him a nice facility designed for the elderly. He said he was happy to have a home but his actions spoke differently. Every day, even now, he is on the streets, pan handling and sitting in coffee shops talking to people as they come in for their morning libation and snack. He manages, through his kindness, to collect the change from patrons as they cash out their orders. I'm sure they feel badly for him and don't know the "real" story of his life. He doesn't like to be confined and certainly does not like rules or to be told when he can come and go. Despite the fact he has a warm place to sleep each night, the life he chooses is mostly on the streets. For some reason, I'm sure only he really knows why; he likes it this way and will continue to live out the remainder of his life in this manner. The moon will continue to guide and watch over him as he takes charge of how much light he seeks. I was again left questioning the larger point of life and the lessons I was meant to learn from this experience. I didn't then and don't now fully understand the bigger picture. In these moments, I engage my faith to help direct me.

When I was younger, we'd often go to NYC. This was a treat for us children and certainly one for my father who loves to walk the streets of the "big city." I remember seeing homeless people on the streets. They made their homes from cardboard boxes perched on top of heating vents in the sidewalk. I would ask my mother, even as a young child, what this was all about and she would say some people don't have enough money to live in houses or buy food so this was where they lived and slept. I was horrified to think people were forced to live in this way. As an adult having spent 10 years working with this population, I now see why some people actually choose to live this way; I am sure many of them have their reasons for doing so. I am also cognizant that undiagnosed mental health issues play a part in why some choose this option over another. Because all people have the right to choose, whether we agree or not with their decisions, we have to sit back and let the scenario play out. The moon lights the sky for everyone and we all have the option to be guided by it-or not.

My life has been good, fair and for the most part, predictable. Other than basic worries, I never questioned personal safety, self-worth, where I would live or whether there were people in my life I could rely on. It was and always has been a given. My childhood was filled with wonder, memorable experiences and humor, as childhoods should be. I come from a long line of *way* off-Broadway comedians and I grew up in a household where people laughed and found humor in life's major curve balls. This has become part of my personality and my moon. Just to give you an idea of life in my house, let me entertain you with a couple of stories illuminating the fact.

One day my mother received a free sample of a brand new laundry detergent that was making its way on the market. Being the dutiful wife and mother she did a load of whites. We had no clue.

The next day my father goes off to work and my brother, sister and I go off to school; a very typical day in the life of the Mazzeo family. Throughout the morning I found myself scratching my itchy skin. It was an annoying fingernail on the chalkboard kind of itch so I scratched my pink skin to red and still couldn't squelch the annoyance. Before I knew it, my white shirt started falling apart in my hand to the point where the sleeve fell clear off the rest of the shirt. I was in

Elementary School at the time so I did not know what was happening or what to do about it. I was embarrassed and certain everyone noticed my shirt was falling apart before our very eyes. I did what any other level headed little girl would do; I found a sweater and put it on. I can't remember if it was sweater weather or not, but really it didn't matter, I needed covering up!

I found my brother at some point during the day and learned he was having the same issue. We both didn't understand what was going on. Nothing like this had ever happened to us before. When we got home later in the day, we found our sister also shared our experience. She was at a different school so we didn't know she was living her own personal hell. Her clothes, like ours, fell apart. My mother, pretty amazed by what she saw, had no explanation for what clearly was the 8th wonder of the world. She kept babbling about how we all needed new clothes now.

Now I'll fast forward to my poor father; a business man who held a managerial position in a check printing company and was well respected in his career. He found himself scratching the skin off his bones all day long. Of course he was thinking this problem was an isolated one and apparently didn't think to check in with home base to declare the difficulty he was having. The only thing he knew was each time he scratched, another part of his clothing disappeared and he walked around work with tattered and torn clothing. Hours later, when he finally returned home, he threw open the front door and began to call for my mother. The way in which he dragged out the "t" in her name alerted us there were problems in river city. "Jeanetttttttttttt ttttttttttttttttttttttttttttttttttttttttttttttttttttttttttttte, where are you?" We all went to greet him and found a grown man who unzipped his pants in the middle of our hallway exposing tattered boxers with the only thing fully in tact being the elastic waistband! He couldn't stay angry long as we were all laughing hysterically at how pathetic he looked.

When my mother saw he was wearing white clothing, she put two and two together and ran to get the detergent box from the trash...and there it was! Clear as day the instructions indicated the product should not be mixed with bleach. Need I say we never let her live down the faux pas?

Okay, so maybe this was funnier to live through than it is to relate but there was a very important life lesson here: Don't take life too seriously. We learned through experiences like these (and man, there were many), life, with all its unplanned bumps, can consume you if you let it.

One day that started out as all others-like most do, ended very differently. My brother decided to burn the Christmas tree in the fireplace almost setting the entire family room in flames. He had seen my father do this numerous times and perhaps saw this accomplishment as some kind of "rite of passage."

The ironic thing to me is that I (as the youngest) had to instruct my older brother (who was filling up a frying pan with water to throw at the ceiling) and my sister (who was walking around in a circle repeating everything I was saying) as I simultaneously tried to shuffle my young cousins out of the house. Oh, did I mention they were living with us because their home had burned down and they needed temporary shelter? Alright, maybe my siblings have a different version of how the story unfolded but the truth is, with no one hurt and the only damage was a scorched ceiling (something a little muscle and paint could fix) the story is both ironic and funny. My brother gathered two cups of water per trip to and from the kitchen to throw at the burning ceiling, maybe having half of it actually reach the flames when all was said and done. My sister, the oldest of all, couldn't get her thoughts together enough to call the fire department until, yes, you guessed it, I told her too and lastly, my poor cousins were living through yet another house fire. Really, how many fires does one person live through in a lifetime?

The bottom line is I think humor is a gift given to us by others and we pass it on to those we know and love. In this case, my parents and those important to me while growing up were funny people who tried to see the lighter side of life even in situations that didn't start off very funny. In doing so, they taught us the same. When I share my sense of humor with those I care about, I'm giving them a personal gift because my humor is a dimension of my personality. If you want to get to know me, you have to get to know this part of me as well. My humor was developed and cultivated by my family and family friends; very funny people in their own right.

I try and teach humor in my work because I see the important role it can play in the healing process. If people are willing to take a step back for a moment in order to gain perspective from a different vantage point, they might be able to see the levity of a situation. I do this by acting silly, by giving a humorous perspective on the situation and I do this by asking if there is any part of the current situation/obstacle that has a comical twist to it. Of course I do this with sensitivity, as it would never be my intention to make someone feel as though I am undermining them or their experiences in any way. I've seen this technique work time and time again. When kids recognize I am being silly or see that I am looking at things in a slightly different way, they often mirror it. Humor is healing and it has become part of my moon and ability to move forward when circumstances bog me down. For those who know me, it's no secret that if I'm not finding the humorous side of a situation then it is time to intervene because humor is my rote response to problem solving. If I am looking at things too seriously and failing to see the humor, send in the National Guard, I need help!

As I mature and grow older, I find solace and comfort in my personal spiritual beliefs and knowledge of a higher being. The two have caused me to feel more grounded as an individual and enable me to continue on in this work-as I need something to rely on when the going gets tough. The comfort I feel in knowing something greater than I does in fact exist, helps me to bring definition to my moon; my path and my light. It provides strength and it provides fertile ground when my energy level needs restoration. I believe there is something bigger out there. I further believe we are placed in this world and given specific experiences to learn from. I believe we bring the lessons learned from one life into other lives. Some think this concept to be way off the mark but for me it's the only explanation that provides enough possibility. How else can I explain why some have it so easy and others have it so hard? Are there lessons in every experience (good or bad) we are to store subconsciously for further use?

I often wonder how or why I entered a field where every ounce of your soul is called to action. I never even knew social work existed and literally stumbled upon it in college. My lifelong intention was to be a writer, not a social worker. Now that I am a social worker, I can't imagine dedicating my life to anything else. In my mind, no other career could offer this much personal satisfaction and personal growth.

When I began doing research on opportunities in the social work field, my first thought was…. "What, I can get paid for doing something I've been doing all of my life and it doesn't include math?" Just to get you up to speed, I was voted "most dependable" in high school. I was the one-all those years' ago-people felt they could rely on and confide in. I knew the secrets, gave the advice and was the ultimate observer. People fascinated me and I was happy watching how they operated. I still am.

I was just being me-people figured out I was someone who cared and took an interest in listening to whatever they had to say. When I realized I could take those innate skills and put them to use, I was thrilled. This was the career for me and I was going for it.

95

Social work has allowed me to combine my spirituality, the curiosity I have for people and their stories and my ability to make quick and meaningful relationships. I am a safe person and people recognize this in me. It has given me the opportunity to give back what I have so freely been given and it allows me the chance to teach what I have learned to others. In this field, I've learned I have a personal mission and the mission is: ***If you have the capacity to do something for someone else which will make their life easier, then do it.*** Everyone has the right to happiness and to have others care about them.

Spirituality and social work go hand in hand for me. When life continues to provide opportunities to become intimately involved with the lives of others, you have to believe in something greater in order to maintain the courage to move forward with them. There's too much sadness in the world and if you don't know how to let the sadness go or how to put it in its proper place, it will bring you down and render you useless to others. I depend on and call upon my spirituality often to guide me through both good and bad times.

One day I was visiting a young adolescent in the hospital. For some unknown reason she was very talkative and introspective on this particular day. As she related intensely difficult parts of her life, she began to cry. This was a primal cry and one I've rarely (if ever) heard before. It started at her toes and continued into the depths of her soul. The sounds she made traveled through my body like electric shock and her pain echoed in my head. It was agonizing to be with her through this sadness, but it was what she needed most. So I sat and listened.

In the conversation, she indicated the one and only person she ever loved and who supported her most in her life had died and she felt like no one else on this earth could take her place; despite vast attempts by all who cared for her. Her grandmother had passed on and in her leaving; she had taken part of this child with her. The teen was clearly lost and did not know how to find her way back without her grandmother's guidance. I rarely and sparingly bring spirituality into my work and only do so if I assess it to be helpful to the person I am with. Almost innately and without much thought, I said to her, "Did you ever think your grandmother sent us to help you? Did you ever consider in her absence, she sent people in her place to be with you?" Much to my surprise, this was something the youth thought was worth considering as she paused briefly to say this had never occurred to her. She actually considered the possibility of her grandmother sending help the only way she could.

As I left the visit, I hugged this youth a little tighter than I normally would have and secretly hoped my strength and energy would somehow penetrate her body and give her personal strength. I gathered my thoughts and left the building, reviewing my life's gifts with every step I took. Later in the evening while reviewing my day before I fell asleep, I reached out to this girl's grandmother in prayer and asked for her assistance in helping her grandchild. Even I was bright enough to realize all of my clinical training and experience was not enough to turn this girl around. I surrendered to the notion that if I had to call out to those who passed on for help, I was going to do it.

My moon continues to evolve because I am open to all possibilities and I believe there is a greater purpose to my life and the lives of others. We are all connected. I think the lessons we learn in life and through our experiences are not learned in vain. They must hold deeper meaning; often times more than meet the eye. Maybe we aren't meant to fully understand the nuances in this lifetime and maybe still there are opportunities for us to connect the dots so the unexplainable makes an ounce of palatable sense. This enables the human spirit to grow and learn and to constantly move forward.

I've made a conscious decision to believe and therefore I choose to move onward in my personal development. I choose resiliency and I choose the light of moon over the darkness of the night.

# What Defines Resiliency?

### *The energy within enables us*
### *to become who we were meant to be*

I believe resiliency is the end result for a child when someone-usually an adult-lets that child know they are cared for and sees them as valuable. Even when life seems to be falling apart, people need to know there is a light in the harbor and the light is close enough to touch. It's universal. Most human beings need to feel connected to others; it's what the human spirit craves. Connection to others wards off loneliness and heals pain and sorrow. I was, and continue to be, fortunate enough to experience this in my life.

I feel connected to my world and to something bigger than what is within my vision. I have people in my life circle who care about me and people who I can call if I need help. I am also a person people call when they need help. It's a reciprocity found in any solid, healthy relationship and it's the building block which continues to bring strength to the relationship.

I always had a "best" friend. In high school, I had three: Kim, Diane and Kathie. We were there for one another and the mutual support helped us to navigate the sometimes difficult stressors associated with peer relationships, growing up and family life.

There was never a moment in time when I didn't feel particularly connected to someone whom I thought was special and who thought I was special in return.

This is a tremendous self-esteem builder and attributes to why I feel like a grounded and solid person. In my early years I learned this from family and from my parents. Because I did, when it was time to venture into the world as an independent person I took the skills with me and capitalized on the foundation already laid. When I spend time with my brother and sister and their families, I am connected to their lives because we share common experiences-because of our experiences we "get" each other. This is comforting. I store these moments in my psyche for the days that are difficult to get through. I feel resilient because I know I don't walk this life alone. Most of the children I work with can't say this. They've lived in many homes and have had many families so it's difficult, if not impossible, for them to feel truly connected or special to anyone.

I met Trish when she was five years old. She and her siblings were dropped off at the agency by their birth mother. Their birth mother asked us to care for them because she simply could not do it any longer and needed our help. Unknown to Trish and me at the time, that day was the beginning of a lifelong relationship for us. Employed by the agency, I was her social worker and I placed her in three different foster homes. When I left the agency, I was contracted by them to provide individual therapy for her and when she reached adulthood and returned to her mother's care (by Trish's choice) I remained a positive adult in her life. Approximately 20 years have passed since our first meeting and I have seen her graduate from high school, from college and enter the work force as a full time employee. We see each other, speak often and when she needs a hand or someone to talk with, she calls me.

What started as a routine conversation one day not too long ago ended as an eye opening one for me. She asked me if I realized I was the most consistent adult she had in her life. Although I hadn't really thought about it, I was touched our connection meant enough to her for her to mention it to me. She could see her words left an obvious impact and was surprised I didn't realize how important I was to her. When I tried to explain how happy I was to be a significant person in her life and to have her in mine, she giggled. When I asked what was funny, she said "You don't even know, do you? Well, if you're surprised at this, you'll be really surprised to hear you'll be the one walking me down the aisle at my wedding!" Again, everyone needs to feel connected in life in order to feel valued and special. I guess you can say we are both guided by the moon's light. We each broadened our personal resilience through one another's care and concern.

There weren't any "Friendship 101" courses offered in my 18 years of schooling. These were lessons received from life and "teachers" came in many forms. They were your friends, relatives, school teachers, doctors and anyone else who entered your world and took an interest in you. This elite group of people also helped define who you were as a person because they recognized the strengths and weaknesses you possessed. People continuously share their observations of you (whether or not you ask them to do so) and these observations force you to take a look at the information they lay out. Because once information hits the air, it's out there and you HAVE to pay attention to it. There is always validity in another person's observation, even if you don't agree 100%. A person who looks at life as one big lesson is willing, at the very least, to hear out another person.

Early on in my career a co-worker, who was much older than I, made a passing statement to me which was both infuriating and tremendously life-changing. I made some snide comment (snide comments were well within my immature rights because I wasn't operating with full brain capacity at 23!) about someone not getting back to me in a timely fashion. Obviously being big and bad and never making any errors myself, I commented that this person had some nerve keeping me waiting for as long as she had. My co-worker, as a result of my comment, nicely pointed out it was too bad I had to judge everyone else's behavior based on my own definitions and she found it sad I never cut anyone slack for the minor imperfections they might have. WELL, you could have driven a dagger through my heart. How in God's name could this woman sit and call me judgmental. *ME, ME?* She called *ME* judgmental? Why, I was the fairest person I knew!

After I took considerable time to swallow my pride and lick my wounds I realized, with every fiber of my physical make up, she was absolutely correct in her observation of my inexcusable behavior. I had no right expecting things from people they just couldn't deliver. If I chose to behave or react in a certain manner then this was my choice. If someone didn't do something the way I wanted them to it wasn't their problem, it was mine. I learned a valuable and meaningful lesson about myself on this day and I look back on it each time I feel I'm running out of patience with people. Congratulations to her, she probably said aloud what others were thinking. I was a judgmental brat and someone had to call me out on my behavior.

Growing up in my family, people were painfully verbal when they thought you were acting like an idiot and they were the first to let you know when you were making poor choices. Maybe this is why it's easier to hear the good and bad about myself now. I'm used to it. If we made a dumb, thoughtless, ah, shall we say error in judgment, my mother let us know about it for hours on end. We would have done anything to take it back, just to quiet her down. She was a self-proclaimed yeller and this was the worst punishment of all. She yelled, she screamed, she yelled, she screamed and she yelled some more in case you didn't get the message the first 8,000 times she said it! You know what's amusing? I remember the yelling less and the fact I was always forgiven, more. I knew no matter what stupid thing I did, it didn't make me any less loveable to my parents. This IS NOT to say you weren't going to hear about it **forever.**

Here's a less serious example to bring the point home. Within months of getting my driver's license at 16, I was driving my mother to work and I crashed my father's brand new car into a telephone pole. My father was on a business trip out of town at the time and had to hear the news from my older sister. Thankfully my mother and I were okay and the largest bruise I got was the one to my ego. She, on the other hand, had to pick windshield glass out of her hair for days.

When my father called home on the day it happened, my sister had to let him know his new car was no longer among the living. She started by saying, "Dad, Mommy and Lisa were in a car accident." I'm not sure if he first asked if we were ok. What I do know is he asked, "With your car, Debbie (which was something like a 1919 Pontiac)?" My sister informed him, "No dad, your car." He says, "With the Pinto?" and she repeated, "With your car, Dad." He asked again (just for clarification, I'm sure…..), "Was she driving your car?" and again my poor sister had to say, "Dad, Lisa was driving your brand new car and it's totaled."

We have had many good laughs over this story through the years because it's easy to poke fun at things which are slightly unresolved as a way of dealing with them. I felt awful I totaled his brand new car- I couldn't forgive myself for it. Even though I couldn't, my parents did and this was the message I received from them. Their unconditional love and forgiveness is what helped me get through the guilt.

These are the lifetime experiences that provide us with resilience and we never know how valuable they are and the indelible marks they leave until years later when we reflect upon them.

We make mistakes and people forgive us. We can't forgive ourselves and others remind us we are human, loveable and forgivable. We say dumb things and, make judgmental statements, we learn, through those who love us that we are human and humans make mistakes each and every day. People in our lives define us and help us to understand who we are and what we are made of. It's the beauty of having people in our lives taking a risk and sharing their observations, all because they love us. The safety of these caring relationships softens the blow and we begin to understand, regardless of our mistakes, we are forgiven and we are loved. These actions help to create resiliency and define personality.

Resiliency is the life jacket that keeps us afloat through difficult times. It is the result of someone reaching out their hand and grabbing hold of us. The unconditional messages help us to understand we are good, we are worthy and we are capable.

The children and youth I work with do not share this same foundation and spend a lifetime trying to define who they are. They didn't have adults who held onto them for dear life and helped them to develop a sense of self. When we lack true connection and unconditional love, we lack foundation and solid footing. If we lack stability, in my opinion, there is little chance to develop resiliency and self-reliance.

# Suicide

*On this day of "life meets death" inertia,*
*I wish you peace as you continue your journey*

Taking one's own life leaves a hole so enormous in those left behind mere words become inadequate. The guilt felt by survivors is immeasurable and often inconsolable. People who choose suicide do so because they feel helpless and hopeless. Depression, a serious mental illness, is to blame in most cases. I believe adult suicide and childhood suicide is different. Though it would be nearly impossible to prove, I strongly believe children commit suicide out of impulse and because they don't understand finality like adults do. A child's sense of cause and affect are obviously very different than that of an adult. Thus, when they are having a bad time of it, they just want to end the pain but have no way of comprehending end means end when you do drastic things. Developmentally, children don't fully comprehend cause and effect. This is a concept understood as one gets much older.

Did you ever ask a child what they think happens to people after they die? Their answers vary from "I don't know" to "People go to heaven." When you ask what heaven is like, their answers vary even further. It's hard for them to articulate finality because they likely do not understand it in its full capacity.

In this field, it is likely you will deal with suicide in one way or another. In many instances, you will deal with children who talk of suicide often, either as a way to gain attention or as a way to articulate their deep sadness in life. Regardless of the reason, talk of suicide is never to be taken lightly and a full suicidal evaluation must be conducted in order to assess safety risks.

While treating an adolescent in my private practice, she referred to a friend who kept talking about taking her life. She was concerned and didn't quite know how to handle the situation. Due to the seriousness of it she asked my opinion. I tried to gather as much information from her as possible which she hesitantly provided. She felt an alliance to her friend yet, for obvious reasons, she couldn't carry this burden alone. She was in a precarious position; wanting to do the right thing but not wanting to betray her friend's trust.

It was difficult to ascertain whether her friend was truly considering suicide or was simply reaching out for help as I didn't know the friend and had never spoken with her directly. I concluded it was both. By the third week of this, I decided I couldn't hold onto the information any longer without trying to reach out. Since I only had limited information to go on, it was like finding a needle in a haystack. I proceeded along with what I had and made some calls to others I thought could help. We located the youth and learned this was a serious situation. The youth had a knife and a note. It was a matter of time before she was going to take action and take her life.

The youth was hospitalized and treated. Weeks later, I received a call from the father of this child. He started by saying, "You don't know me but I want to thank you for saving my daughter." If I had not taken this seriously, I shudder to think what might have happened for this youth and her family. Maybe it was my time to absorb the light of the moon and maybe this was one of those times where I was the conduit of "divine intervention." However you'd like to interpret it, I was glad I listened and took the necessary action for the overall good.

I've treated siblings of children who've committed suicide, known family survivors of suicide victims and counseled children whose parents ended their lives. The common thread in all of the scenarios is the desperation, deep agonizing pain and unanswered questions left behind. The only people who know the "real" answers are the ones who chose death over life and this leaves open wounds and slow to mend scars for the people who loved them. It's devastating and only time can help to ease the pain. It's one thing to mourn the loss of a loved one who has died from a disease of which they had no control. It's completely different to mourn the loss of someone you didn't know was dying in silence, the guilt of not knowing why this happened is all consuming.

Talk or thoughts of suicide should be fully explored. Never assume that what you are hearing does not require further conversation. It does. Don't ignore warning signs and make it your business to seek further assistance when necessary. Mental health professionals are the only ones qualified when determining a person's level of personal safety.

# To Err is Human, Not Learning "the" Lesson is the True Mistake

*Mistakes are life's way of reminding us we are not perfect. Consider them an opportunity for growth*

Making mistakes is expected and it's a fact of life that all humans make mistakes. What we do with the lessons learned is an entirely different situation. As clinicians, as parents, as people, we stumble and fall, until we've mastered a certain skill. The funny thing about life is "the falls" provide opportunities for us to learn the lessons we need to learn-we keep falling until we learn them. Did you ever find yourself saying "Why does this keep happening to me?" The truth of the matter is, "it" keeps happening because we refuse to take a hard look at the situation(s) and what we are supposed to be learning from these experiences. We get stuck in a behavioral pattern that becomes circular. We spin and we spin until we finally stop the pattern and make changes.

I wouldn't have admitted it at the time but I'm proud to say I've made mistakes personally and professionally; too many to count. Inevitably, it wasn't until I took a step back that I was able to understand if I didn't change my behavior, attitude, style, the results would remain the same. When I started making slow changes, one change at a time, I was able to break my personal cycle and move on.

Adolescents are notorious for staying stuck in their limited beliefs and ways. They don't even know what they don't know but will argue a point until you want to scream. They get fixated and refuse to change their ways because their stubbornness and personal limitations get in their way. Yes folks, we are dealing with "unfinished" brains. Teenagers remind us of this through such behavior. In order to contain my own frustration and bring a little humor to the situation when teens refuse to budge, I strategically comment…"Ah, you don't know what you're talking about. You only have half a brain." This quiets them down for a minute and allows us the opportunity to regroup.

The youth I work with do this tenfold. They have maladaptive behaviors and continue using them until the cows come home. I'm of the belief the chosen behavior is a coping mechanism which has worked well for them in their mission of survival. They begin on shaky ground and continue in this way until someone stronger than them stops them in their tracks. They know no better and will fight you to the bitter end. You have to be bigger and stronger than them in order to facilitate a pattern change.

Years ago I was assigned the case of a 13 year-old girl. She was street smart, guarded from all that could potentially hurt her and had developed a personality style which was bitter and caustic. Needless to say, she wasn't easy or fun to be around. The State had custody of her so I had to see her often and each time I had to go, I dreaded it. She used her snarky personality to make me uncomfortable and keep me distant and I knew this but couldn't change it. Each time I made a date to see her, I'd give a specific time, day, location etc. and each time I went, she wouldn't be there. She never was where she said she would be so I would end up having to drive around until I finally caught up with her. When I did, she'd give me the third degree. "Why do you keep finding me, why do I have to see you all the time, you're not in charge of me, blah, blah, blah"...you get the idea. This infuriated me (exactly the reaction she was looking for) because I'm thinking I'm going out of my way to ensure her safety and she's blocking my every attempt. She knew it and she did it more. She was testing me and I was falling for it. I was letting my ego get in the way of building the relationship even though my ego had nothing to do with what was going on. This child was simply acting out of instinct and I was reacting to it. This went on until I finally came to my senses. It suddenly occurred to me she was pushing me away because she had been pushed aside by every adult she's ever known, starting with her mother. When I put this piece of the puzzle together, the relationship shifted and I learned, just because I knew I was a loyal and dependable person, it didn't mean she knew it. Why would she? She had few positive role models in life? My lesson: Don't let yourself get in the way of relationships. People are who they are and they will come around in their own time. Our only responsibility to someone else is to be who we are. It's the best gift we can offer and it's genuine.

I'm happy to say this girl eventually realized I did what I promised, showed up when I said I would and asked little in return of her. When she was mature enough to talk about it, she admitted she was scared to get close to anyone because the times when she allowed herself to do so, people took advantage of her and she wasn't going to let it happen again. She had personally vowed not to subject herself to this kind of pain again and she was determined to adhere to the promise she made to herself. When I asked her what turned her around, she was able to say she spent a lot of time watching my actions. She said she got tired of fighting and thought she might want to try something different. She didn't hesitate to tell me I miserably failed her initial tests! (Ah, thanks for the encouragement...I knew this already!)

Maybe I helped steer her in the direction of her moon; a moon she didn't even know she was missing in her life and maybe I did this just by being who I am.

One of the adolescents in my private practice was talking about her pregnancy and how scared she was about it. She briefly mentioned abortion but did not make this the topic of our discussion. Rather, she wanted to address her fear of being pregnant. Instead of being with her in the moment, I jumped right back to the abortion alternative. The look of disappointment on her face told me I had disregarded her feelings and moved directly into a conversation she clearly wasn't ready to have. I was initially taken back by her response until I thought a minute about her reaction. She was right and I was wrong. I had no business trying to get her to talk about something she was not ready to discuss. She put me in my place when she said, "How could you bring up abortion with me, I am NOWHERE near there yet!" When I look back at the scenario, I know I let my own anxiety get in the way of my being in the moment with her. If I had carried on with how I thought the scenario should have played out, I would have deprived her of her process, her right to decide and her moon; her guiding light.

Luckily she and I had a solid relationship and she was able to cut me a little slack on this one. If we didn't have a good therapeutic bond, this could have caused the relationship to abruptly end because I can't think of any person, let alone a client, who would want the person they are confiding in to be judgmental or make suggestions about major life decisions.

A solid therapeutic alliance is what will save a client/therapist relationship, just as a strong relationship between a parent and a child will ultimately save the relationship during difficult times. I can't speak enough about the importance of creating solid relationships that stand the test of time. They will ultimately be your life jacket when treatment or basic parenting isn't going well. People are willing to give you a break when they believe your intentions are for their greater good.

As mentioned earlier, my mother was a yeller. This is how she released her frustration, disappointment, anger and anxiety. As kids, we learned this was she. I can't say it was easy to take, but we did so because we knew our mother loved us and in some odd way, her yelling was a sign of it. The point is we cut her slack for her imperfections as she cut us slack for ours. It was all part of the relationship; a relationship which was solid, consistent and predictable; basic building blocks for a sturdy foundation. I learned early we are all imperfect beings and through our imperfections, we learn tolerance and compassion for others. It's a value I stand by today.

Skill acquisition takes observation, trial and error. When a toddler is learning to walk, he goes forward four steps, falls back two, goes forward one, then back three, until he finally masters the skill and walks without assistance or support. We need to be patient until people get to where they need to be even though standing on the sidelines during difficult times isn't always easy. If you interfere with a person's personal process, they will never achieve whatever it is they are trying to master; their lesson, their path. We can guide and we can make connections but we cannot interfere. It's their life, their journey.

If you work with or raise children they will tell you, in no uncertain terms, you are crossing boundaries with them. Heed the warning. I'm not saying parents shouldn't be involved with their children's lives and I'm not saying clinicians shouldn't address painful territory with clients. I am saying you have to carefully tread the waters if you are to have an impact. People have to learn in their own time, utilizing their own experiences and internal resources. If we consistently give the answers then they don't learn problem-solving skills. Everyone is going to fall. The question is will you be there to help them up?

# Self-care and All that Related Jazz

I really **DO** believe "self-care" is an over-rated and over used term in today's society. However, I wholeheartedly believe in the message. Realizing you must take a break when you need to and splurging on something which makes you feel good are not only necessities in life but suggest you know yourself well enough to do so. I think any parent or person would agree you need a break from life every now and again; regardless of how much you love your life, children and family. Our minds yearn for quiet from time to time and quiet is what we should find.

The human services field is different than most others as it consistently taps into the entirety of who you are. When I go into work each day, I am not adding cogs to a wheel; I'm helping others understand themselves and this takes focus and emotional energy. Though vastly rewarding, it can be exhausting as well.

I've worked in the restaurant business, have done factory work and have worked in retail. Even though these are physically draining, sometimes mind numbing careers, I find the field of social services to be unique in that it is emotionally taxing. Consequently, I've learned to find ways to replenish my soul in order to face what lies ahead.

I am a fundamental believer happiness isn't a thing and you can't buy it; it's a feeling of peace derived from experiences. If I give myself permission to become immersed in my feelings and their meanings, I am restored. I've further realized I have to give ample time to exploring my "quiet self" in order to maintain personal equilibrium.

Through research, I've learned I am an "Ambivert". In the world of Meyer's Briggs Personality testing, you are determined to be either Introvert or Extrovert. To summarize an extremely extensive assessment tool, Extroverts are externally motivated and Introverts are internally motivated. Another term, "Ambivert," indicates you typically fall within the middle. My mood during a particular timeframe determines whether internal or external factors contribute to recharging my battery. Sometimes I need people around while other times I need quiet to nurture my own thoughts. If I don't achieve this balance, I get cranky and I know it. If I know it, you'll know it too. Since acting cranky is not what I choose to do, I have to pay attention to what I need and when. This becomes part of my self-care routine.

I've always been a lover of music and this has come to be one of the ways I reduce stress. I'm sure you will agree that the creation of the "play list" was the greatest invention ever! Music relentlessly touches my soul; sometimes by purposeful planning and sometimes by sheer accident. I can get lost in lyrics and if the musical notes flow nicely with them, I'm a goner. I think the written and spoken language is poetic in and of itself and if you are astute enough to know how to connect them together with musical notes, it reaches the minds and souls of others.

I remember a day when my father, also a lover of music, played a musical video of the song "Starry, Starry Night" for me. He had heard it and knew it was something I'd appreciate listening to. If you are familiar with this song's meaning then you already understand it was written about Vincent van Gogh and the emotional struggles he endured during his lifetime. This three or four minute song captured the essence of Vincent, a clearly talented yet tortured soul. It was profound enough to make me cry and beautiful enough to make me smile. The video choreographer clearly touched emotional places in me which are typically too weighed down by everyday life stress to access. If not for taking time to listen, I might forget about this particular dimension of who I am.

Moments such as the one exampled above are absolute musts in my life and I am saddened when I see others don't have experiences like these to reflect upon. I am not intimating everyone needs to get from one place to the next in exactly the same way. I am, however, implying we all need to find our "place of solace" if we are to grow as individuals. Many children and youth, especially in today's technological world, have not been taught to find internal happiness and peace but rather, spend their time seeking immediate gratification in an attempt to meet their immediate needs. Couple this with the absence of early childhood nurturance, spiritual grounding and unconditional love and you have someone who feels lost and without grounding. This, as they say, is a recipe for disaster. Learning to explore the depths of who you are is a skill;

it must be taught and practiced as it rarely comes to us naturally.

I use music in my work and I've learned its clinical usefulness in therapy sessions (thanks to my friend Jayme who allowed this to be the central focus of our work together years ago). I have it playing in my car while driving alone or with a child, I use it in teaching and I use it to increase my calm. I believe music to be "the" universal language and I feel people connect as human beings through it. At some point in life, who hasn't been able to let a song whisk them away to places unknown? I think it helps the non-verbal person, or those who have difficulty accessing their feelings, to understand how their mind, body and soul are connected. These activities have become an integral part of "my moon" because they help to shed personal light on my capacity as a human being and are the fuel which keeps my system running smoothly.

Listening to music, walks on the beach or gardening are all tools I use to focus myself. All three give me permission to get lost within myself for a moment or two and thus are my attempts at self-care. During these peaceful moments, I allow myself to dissect my own thoughts, understand my body cues and realize my feelings. I can think, I can problem solve, I can make sense of things which are hard to explain, I can dream and I can replenish my personal reservoir so I am able to face another challenge.

Teaching this to others is important yet not always easy. Many children and youth make either overt or covert decisions to close off their feelings. This can occur as a result of the unspeakable things which have been done to them. Or because hurt from past experiences is so deeply felt the only obvious choice for them was to stop the pain. Whatever the reason for their decision, when we meet, our task is to develop a plan to learn how to regain acknowledgment of their feeling state. For some, the concept of understanding why we feel the way we feel is a foreign one and accepting "feeling states" as another dimension of ourselves is not a priority.

My young friend Patrice is an example of this. Though she came from a very loving and supportive divorced family, I believe the resulting pain from the divorce caused her to shut down this particular aspect of who she was. Though it is reasonable to assume she had feelings, she didn't acknowledge them and frankly thought she had no use for them. Her feelings would build up and she subconsciously tucked them away until, for no seemingly good reason, she would react to benign situations and not understand why her reactions were so severe. It's rarely the benign situation that yields a reaction but rather the proverbial "straw that broke the camel's back" that is the culprit. In our work together, though she challenged me each step of the way, she needed to understand human nature and how reactions to situations in life, either knowingly or unknowingly, happen. Recognizing body cues and learning how to pick up on them is a difficult but necessary exercise for balanced mental wellness. If you don't know how to innately do this then we have to teach the skill and understanding it becomes perfected through practice. Most times while teaching this to adolescents, they look at you as though you have 15 eyes. They are typically disconnected from their body and honestly do not understand how to connect harmoniously with it. When they begin to see positive changes as a result of doing painless exercises like nightly emotional body scans (how does each part of my body feel as I lay here), listening to music, and allowing quiet in their lives, they are more apt to continue practicing.

Self-care is important and should be included in your daily routine. If we don't pay close attention to our body cues then we don't understand our reactions to the many things we face on a daily basis. Our reactions to situations (good or bad) are not random acts. Reactions are the body's way of alerting us that we must pay attention and make adjustments in order for a healthy balance to be achieved.

# Finding Your Groove

*Whatever the dance, enjoy the gracefulness of music*

Musicians, writers and all other creative types must find the style of their art. It is true for the therapist as well. Without style, it's difficult to set the course for your work. Personal style creates uniqueness, sets you apart from the masses and creates direction.

I stumbled upon my style. I didn't know I was looking for it nor did I know I developed it until others pointed it out to me. Unsolicited feedback causes you to look at what you are doing and I remember the first moment I took pause and listened.

I was working in a child welfare agency at the time. I knew I gravitated toward adolescents; mostly because I enjoyed being in their presence. Secretly, I think it "really" was because I didn't feel much older than them even though I was old enough to be their mother (or at the very least their older sister)! We were planning a weekend life skills development program where we would take the foster youth away for two nights and teach independent and social skills. When staff was determining what our specific roles would be in the program curriculum, my supervisor said, "Give that part to Lisa, she's great with teenagers. She makes quick relationships with them." I had no idea (1.) This was true and (2.) Anyone had noticed this strength in me. As a result, I was able to identify this strength as one of my skills moving forward. Hence my ability to develop "quick relationships" became part of my style. I focused on this and tried to perfect what it meant in the therapeutic alliance.

The next time I was made aware of a stylistic approach is when I was conversing with a good friend years ago about my work. I told her I was afraid I would be out of business when I got older because my work centered on adolescents. I was fearful the day would come when they no longer related to me because of my age. I was scared they wouldn't want to confide in me anymore because I'd no longer be one of them, but rather some old person. Without a second to spare, she responded, "Um, you're old now (I was in my late 30's) and they talk to you!" I was so stunned by what she said because, again, I didn't feel old in my head and if I didn't feel it then surely I wasn't. But, alas, to a 13 year old 39 is pretty old and she was right! My friend pointed out it was my ability to listen and not judge which enabled children to confide in me, not my age. Children know I like and understand them, so this is why they relate to me. I'm not intimidated by their behavior and they feel a sense of safety in my presence. This approach was obviously working and I began to understand this to be part of my style. So as in any craft, I began to hone the skill and make it a conscious and unique part of my approach.

I've had parents and teens alike tell me I'm hard to pull things over on and I don't sugar coat situations. This is one of the reasons they keep coming back. Because this is true in my personal life as well, it wasn't very difficult transitioning this into my practice.

I've come to learn this to be the most beneficial skill to have when working with teenagers, as they are typically a hard sell. They seem to sniff out genuine concern within seconds and if you don't hook them from the start, it's likely the relationship won't progress forward. Genuine concern for others isn't something you can fake and is likely an innate skill which you take with you into your work. If it is absent or fabricated, you won't get beyond the first session. If you are too wrapped up in thinking you have to have the correct response for everything heard then you will get lost in your own head and not listen to what is being said. Those you work with will clearly see through this and begin to recognize you are not "in it" with them. Clients will shut down and give you nothing to work with and likely will not return.

Every individual situation requires you to do a "dance" and the dance you choose becomes a part of your groove and style. It is up to the clinician to determine which dance is suitable for which situation. There are slow dances and there are dances that move much faster. If you choose the incorrect one at a crucial moment then you lose the moment and the client will feel as though you weren't properly reading their cues and it's true. Everyone must go through their process and you can't rush it or skip important aspects of it. The client determines the speed and the clinician follows the lead. In this scenario the dance steps can move from slow to fast to slow again and continue in this way until the client makes the necessary connections.

I learned this the hard way but thankfully I learned it. If you pay attention, clients will tell you when you are moving too fast or too slow. If you recall the story of the adolescent who became pregnant, she was quite clear I was dancing the Salsa and she was doing the Box Step. If I had continued in this way, I would have lost her. I learned something valuable regarding my practice and personality. I am a results oriented person and my lack of patience for her process obviously could have gotten in the way of her right to decide her life. If she hadn't stopped me, I would not have been helpful to her growth. If she chose not to return, I would have been to blame. This lesson taught me even if I think I know where we need to end; the client needs to bring us there, not me. I do the dance; their dance, their pace, their lead. Learning the difference taught me a little about my style as a practitioner.

Using my humor and playfulness as an assessment tool has become stylistic and I've developed this technique through the years. When I am meeting a child/youth for the first time, I typically shake their hand, introduce myself and begin talking to them about random things. I take the child's hand and continue shaking it for more than a minute. As we are shaking hands, I am looking into their eyes and assessing their eye contact and comfort level, I introduce myself and assess whether they introduce themselves in return. I ask questions about who they are as I assess whether they are able to communicate with me in an age appropriate manner. Eventually the child comes to realize I haven't let go of their hand and in this realization, I am able to determine their level of humor. If the child is able to understand I am being playful with them they laugh and this tells me they have the capacity to engage in a playful manner. Within the first five minutes of our meeting and without the child even realizing, I've determined the type of child they are and which course of action I will take with them. I've learned to trust my instincts because they've proved correct more often than not. I know I only have one chance at a first impression and if I blow the chance, the child can decide not to return.

Finding my groove has been synonymous with finding my moon. My groove is part of my professional self and is the road map for my work. Style acquisition comes with experience and practice and cannot be rushed. Like any other developmental milestone achievement you attempt to master, you stumble and fall. Experience, trial and error and work will perfect it over time.

# Mental Health in Children

Undiagnosed and under treated mental health issues in children lead to undiagnosed and under treated mental health issues in adults and as a result, the cyclical epidemic continues. I would be remiss if I didn't speak briefly about this topic before ending this book.

As I write, the State of Connecticut braces itself for the one-year anniversary of the Sandy Hook Elementary School massacre, which resulted in the brutal murder of 20 children and six adults by a young man named Adam Lanza. As the investigation of this unspeakable event unfolds, we are learning about the alleged mental illness of the shooter. Looking back at other such events, mental health seems to be behind these incidents which, should have never happened.

Many school massacres have occurred prior to this one; Columbine and Virginia Tech to name a few. Legislators and politicians continue to argue stricter gun control would prevent situations like these from occurring again. This bottomless topic has been in the eye of the nation for years with little to no resolution.

In my opinion, gun control is one part of a much larger, much more devastating problem. Undiagnosed and under treated mental health issues are the culprit as far as I am concerned.

Anyone in the field can speak intelligibly about a client they have worked with who has been under treated or dismissed from proper mental health care prematurely or has refused proper treatment under their civic right to decide. In-patient, long term hospital stays have been cut short for various reasons- likely due to budget cuts and insurance regulations, though we convince ourselves the goal of community integration is the reason we cut treatment short. Where I'm an advocate for community integration when appropriate, some people simply cannot live in our communities or become part of mainstream society. They can't.

Years ago a colleague and I evaluated a child who was four at the time. This child had a horrific early history filled with abuse and neglect. He was showing early signs of behavior dysregulation and developmental delay. We knew the family well due to the extensive issues they presented with and the frequency of their requests for help. When the evaluation concluded, my colleague and I looked at each other because we knew this child was showing serious signs of mental illness. Due to his age it was necessary to use benign childhood diagnoses to describe his difficulties however, it seemed clear to us his emotional and developmental trajectory would be seriously impaired as he aged.

He spent most of his life in and out of treatment facilities which were designed to address his specific needs. Intensive therapeutic milieus led to less intensive treatment facilities until he ended up in a facility designed for independent living. Journalistic accounts of his story describe how he, along with friends, ran from the independent living home and went, unaccompanied, into the community. These youth, who clearly required additional therapeutic intervention at a level much higher than they were receiving, were on their own during the AWOL. The long and short of the story is he was held responsible for the murder of one of the youth who ran with him. Furthermore, the details of the murder made your skin crawl.

Learning about this incident years later made me physically ill. I'm not sure what went wrong and when or how the system failed this child but I'm certain it did. I realize he is responsible for his actions but his state of mental wellness was seriously compromised when he was very young and did not improve with time. In fact, it worsened to the point of murder. I believe there are two victims here, this youth and the murdered girl.

Could we have prevented this from happening? I have no idea. The only thing I do know is his mental illness was no secret, even as a young boy. Perhaps the extent of his damaged brain is what surprised us when we saw what he was capable of. I'm not sure what happened to his moon because life clearly went dark and reaching for something you can't see is nearly impossible.

There aren't enough specialized facilities to care for and treat those with serious mental illness. The structures that remain are overburdened and understaffed; a recipe for failure and a clear indication as to why some slip through the cracks. In addition, denial of the problem and refusal of treatment by the client add to the reasons why some people go untreated.

I understand this yet it doesn't make it any easier to accept.

Every mental health diagnosis does not lead to erratic, sociopathic behavior. This is the extreme. The list of diagnoses is extensive and the symptoms vary from mild to severe. However, serious mental illness is recognizable by service professionals and behavior can be fairly predictable based on symptomatology and historical patterns of the individual. When you are faced with fight after fight to get the needed treatment for your client, it's infuriating to say the least and easy to give up. Don't give up. Keep fighting for what you know to be correct. Day after day the world has experienced the outcome of untreated mental illness. Is it too much to ask for us to learn our lessons once and for all, so additional prevention sources can be identified and funded and further tragedies avoided?

Mental health is a serious societal problem which must be addressed sooner rather than later in our world or the murderous events will continue. I realize the problem is far greater and much more complicated than what can be discussed here. Experts and scholars have been tackling this issue for decades. Unfortunately, we are running out of time and society's priorities are getting lost.

Yes to gun control and yes to increased mental health treatment. The moon is clearly lost within the clouds in reference to this particular issue and in order for us to progress forward, radical changes must take place to address rather than mask the true problem.

# About the Author

Lisa A. Mazzeo holds a bachelor and master's degree in social work from Southern Connecticut State University and aside from being a social worker, she is a freelance writer and poet gaining inspiration from all the children who have become part of "the system" and whose voices may get lost. Lisa is a member of the National Association of Social Workers (NASW), is a licensed clinical social worker (LCSW) and a Board Certified Diplomat (BCD).

Lisa began her career as a social worker for the State Department of Children and Families (DCF). From there she went to work as a therapist at the Cornell Scott Hill Health Center, as a social worker (then Team Leader) with Casey Family Services, as the Senior Clinician at St. Francis Home for Children, as the Clinical Director at Operation Hope and finally as a Clinical Manager in foster care at Family and Children's Agency. Lisa opened her private practice in 1989 where she specializes in working with adolescents and provides clinical supervision for social workers who are preparing for their licensing exam.

In addition to the above, Lisa has trained professionals and foster parents on the art of parenting foster children, was an adjunct professor at Southern Connecticut State University and was appointed by Senate Minority Leader, Senator John Mckinney, to the state's Commission On Nonprofit Health and Human Services.

Lisa currently resides in East Haven, Connecticut. Her home is a stone's throw from the beach where she often spends her free time watching the moon perform its magic on the ebb and flow of the tide.

Please contact Lisa at whocancatchthemoon.com

CPSIA information can be obtained at www.ICGtesting.com
Printed in the USA
BVOW11s1124260614

357342BV00011B/364/P